LAND LAW

3rd edition

John Duddington
Worcester College of Technology

Longman
is an imprint of

Harlow, England • London • New York • Boston • San Francisco • Toronto • Sydney • Singapore • Hong Kong
Tokyo • Seoul • Taipei • New Delhi • Cape Town • Madrid • Mexico City • Amsterdam • Munich • Paris • Milan

Pearson Education Limited
Edinburgh Gate
Harlow
Essex CM20 2JE
England

and Associated Companies throughout the world

Visit us on the World Wide Web at:
www.pearsoned.co.uk

First published 2007
Second edition 2009
Third edition published 2011

ISBN 978-1-4082-3993-3

British Library Cataloguing-in-Publication Data
A catalogue record for this book is available from the British Library

Library of Congress Cataloging-in-Publication Data
Duddington, John.
    Land law / John Duddington. -- 3rd ed.
        p. cm.
    Includes index.
    ISBN 978-1-4082-3993-3 (pbk.)
    1. Land tenure--Law and legislation--England--Outlines, syllabi,
etc. 2. Land tenure--Law and legislation--Wales--Outlines, syllabi,
etc. I. Title.
    KD833.D83 2010
    346.4204'3--dc22

                                                2010024145

10 9 8 7 6 5 4 3 2
14 13 12 11

Typeset by 3 in 10pt Helvetica Condensed
Printed by Ashford Colour Press Ltd., Gosport

Contents

Supporting resources

Visit the *Law Express Series* companion website at **www.pearsoned.co.uk/lawexpress** to find valuable student learning material including:

Companion Website for Students

- A study plan test to assess how well you know the subject before you begin your revision, now broken down into targeted study units
- Interactive quizzes with a variety of question types to test your knowledge of the main points from each chapter of the book
- Further examination questions and guidelines for answering them
- Interactive flashcards to help you revise the main terms and cases
- Printable versions of the topic maps and checklists
- 'You be the marker' allows you to see exam questions and answers from the perspective of the examiner and includes notes on how an answer might be marked
- Podcasts provide point-by-point instruction on how to answer a common exam question

Also: The companion website provides the following features:

- Search tool to help locate specific items of content
- E-mail results and profile tools to send results of quizzes to instructors
- Online help and support to assist with website usage and troubleshooting

For more information please contact your local Pearson Education sales representative or visit **www.pearsoned.co.uk/lawexpress**.

Acknowledgements

To my father, Walter Duddington, who first encouraged me to become a lawyer, and who would, I think, have enjoyed land law; to my wife Anne, for the constant support, loyalty and technical expertise without which my books would never begin to be written; to my daughter Mary, for her seemingly faultless proofreading and sense of fun which keeps me going, and to my son Christopher for just being himself.

I would also like to thank the staff of Pearson, especially Zoë Botterill and Christine Statham, for their endless encouragement, cheerfulness and practical guidance, and all the reviewers and users of this book who sent in such helpful suggestions for topics which could be included in this edition. I would have been delighted to have adopted more of these but for the limitations of space. However, I do hope that they see at least some of their ideas reflected in the pages of this book.

Finally, readers should know that this book is based on sources available to me at 1 January 2010.

John Duddington
January 2010

■ Publisher's acknowledgements

Our thanks go to all reviewers who contributed to the development of this text, including students who participated in research and focus groups which helped to shape the series format.

Introduction

■ Some general issues

Let us go straight to the point. Students are either land law enthusiasts or they think of it with fear. This book is intended for both types of students as a guide to how to gain the best possible mark in their exams.

Land law enthusiasts will agree that this is one of the most fascinating of all legal subjects. It is rich in variety, full of interesting issues and, more than in some areas of law, of direct relevance to us all.

Students who fear the subject should remember the following points (enthusiasts will find them useful too):

■ There are fewer main cases in land law than in many legal subjects.

■ Land law is more statute based than, for example, contract, tort and equity.

■ The fact that this is so means that there is more certainty, although it also means that you must be able to recall vital statutory provisions accurately.

■ Problem questions are more likely than in some other areas to have a right or wrong answer.

However, there remain two reasons why students do find this subject difficult, and this guide tries to overcome both of them:

1. The language is off-putting. Terms like 'estates' and 'interests' mysteriously subdivide into 'legal' and 'equitable'. Then land registration rules have terms of their own, such as land charges, overriding and minor interests.
2. The structure is difficult to understand: how do the basic ideas of estates and interests fit into the land registration rules, and how do the rules themselves work?

These are particular problems in the material covered in the first two chapters: estates and interests in land and registered and unregistered land. Master these and you will have gone a long way to achieving a reasonable pass in your exam as most questions will involve some knowledge of these areas. Make revision based on these two chapters one of your last jobs before the land law exam.

How does this guide help?

- It takes you through the fundamental areas step by step and encourages you not to go on to the next area until you have mastered the one before.

- It links different areas by revision notes which clearly point you to other linked areas of the syllabus.

- It highlights key cases, statutes and definitions.

- Each chapter has a visual map which clearly shows you how each topic develops.

What this guide *cannot* do is to:

- Do away with the need to learn the material thoroughly and be able to use it in the exam. Only you can do this!

- Act as a substitute for the standard textbooks.

General essay question advice

Answer the actual question and address the issues which it raises. Suppose that you were faced with this question:

'The object of the system of land registration is to ensure that a purchaser will be safe in relying on the register.'

Discuss whether the present system of land registration achieves this aim.

Do not begin by simply describing the system, e.g. by ploughing through minor interests, overriding interests, etc. Essay questions at this level ask for more than this. *This is the most useful tip for success in answering essay questions.*

Then note that the question refers to the present system, i.e. under the Land Registration Act 2002 – you will get credit for pointing this out – and secondly, *deal with the issue posed in the quotation.* You will get more guidance on this both in this book and on the accompanying website. A useful tip is that land law exams often have an essay question on land registration, so have some points ready!

General problem question advice

In answering any problem question follow these steps. This will get your answer off to a good start:

- Identify the right (Chapter 1 gives a list of proprietary and personal rights – memorise them).

- Check whether any interest in the land is legal or equitable.

- Check whether title to the land is registered or unregistered.

This drill applies throughout the subject, e.g. to questions on leases, licences, easements, profits and mortgages. It will not take you all the way but it will give you a good basis.

Ensure that your answer has a good, logical structure leading to a clear conclusion.

■ The 'land law box'

When answering problem questions *always* think of *all* the issues in the box (this is the time to think *inside* the box!):

Legal estates

Legal interests   Equitable interests

Registered title   Unregistered title

Also, make sure you are familiar with these two vital statutes:

- Law of Property Act 1925 – still the foundation of land law terminology – abbreviated to LPA 1925 in this book.
- Land Registration Act 2002 – foundation of the system of land registration – abbreviated to LRA 2002 in this book.

REVISION NOTE

Before you begin, you can use the study plan available on the companion website to assess how well you know the material in this book and identify the areas where you may want to focus your revision.

Guided tour

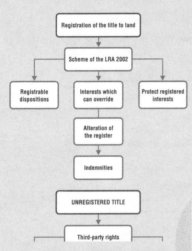

Topic Maps – Visual guides highlight key subject areas and facilitate easy navigation through the chapter. Download them from the companion website to pin to your wall or add to your own revision notes.

Revision Checklist – How well do you know each topic? Use these to identify essential points you should know for your exams. But don't panic if you don't know them all – the chapters will help you revise each point to ensure you are fully prepared for your exams. Print the checklists off the companion website and track your revision progress!

Revision checklist

Essential points you should kno

- [ ] What the terms 'estate', 'freehold'
- [ ] Types of legal interests and equitab
- [ ] When a legal interest binds a third
- [ ] When an equitable interest binds
- [ ] When overreaching can apply ar

Sample Questions – Practice makes perfect! Read the question at the start of each chapter and consider how you would answer it. Guidance on structuring strong answers is provided at the end of the chapter. Try out additional sample questions online.

■ Sample question

Could you answer this question? Below is a typical problem question that could arise on this topic. Guidelines on answering the question are included at the end of this chapter, while a sample essay question and guidance on tackling it can be found on the companion website.

Assessment Advice – Not sure how best to tackle a problem or essay question? Wondering what you may be asked? Be prepared – use the assessment advice to identify the ways in which a subject may be examined and how to apply your knowledge effectively.

ASSESSMENT ADVICE

Essay questions Obvious areas for essay questions are:

- The LRA 2002: how has it changed the system of registered land and how far has it been successful?
- The existence of overriding interests: should they still exist?
- A comparison between the systems of registered and unregistered land.

Problem questions Problem questions may link with other areas or be self-contained. An obvious area to link to is trusts of the home (Chapter 4), where

Don't be tempted to... – Underlines areas where students most often trip up in exams. Use them to avoid making common mistakes and losing marks.

! Don't be tempted to...

Don't assume that you need to come to a definite conclusion on whether a purchaser had notice (especially constructive notice) or not. What is vital is to state the rules clearly and apply them to the facts as far as you can.

Make your answer stand out – Illustrates sources of further thinking and debate where you can maximise your marks. Include these to really impress your examiners!

Key case and key statute boxes – Identify the important elements of the essential cases and statutes you will need to know for your exams.

Key definition boxes – Make sure you understand essential legal terms. Use the flashcards online to test your recall!

Glossary – Forgotten the meaning of a word? This quick reference covers key definitions and other useful terms.

Glossary of terms

The glossary is divided into two parts: key definitions and other useful terms. The key definitions can be found within the chapter in which they occur as well as here, below. These definitions are the essential terms that you must know and understand in order to prepare for an exam. The additional list of terms provides further definitions of useful terms and phrases which will also help you answer examination and coursework questions effectively. These terms are highlighted in the text on their first occurrence but the definition can only be found here.

Key definitions

Exam tips – Feeling the pressure? These boxes indicate how you can improve your exam performance and your chances of getting those top marks!

Revision notes – Highlights related points or areas of overlap in other topics, or areas where your course might adopt a particular approach that you should check with your course tutor.

Guided tour of the companion website

Book resources are available to download. Print your own **topic maps** and **revision checklists!**

Use the **study plan** prior to your revision to help you assess how well you know the subject and determine which areas need most attention. Choose to take the full assessment or focus on targeted study units.

'**Test your knowledge**' of individual areas with quizzes tailored specifically to each chapter. **Sample problem** and **essay questions** are also available with guidance on crafting a good answer.

Flashcards help improve recall of important legal terms and key cases and statutes. Available in both electronic and printable formats.

'You be the marker' gives you the chance to evaluate sample exam answers for different question types and understand how and why an examiner awards marks.

Download the **podcast** and listen as your own personal Law Express tutor guides you through a 10-15 minute audio session. You will be presented with a typical but challenging question and provided a step-by-step explanation on how to approach the question, what essential elements your answer will need for a pass, how to structure a good response, and what to do to make your answer stand out so that you can earn extra marks.

All of this and more can be found when you visit **www.pearsoned.co.uk/lawexpress**

Table of cases and statutes

■ Cases

▉ Statutes

The building
blocks of land law:
estates and interests in land

Revision checklist

Essential points you should know:

☐ What the terms 'estate', 'freehold' and 'leasehold' mean
☐ Types of legal interests and equitable interests in land
☐ When a legal interest binds a third party
☐ When an equitable interest binds a third party
☐ When overreaching can apply and its consequences

Topic map

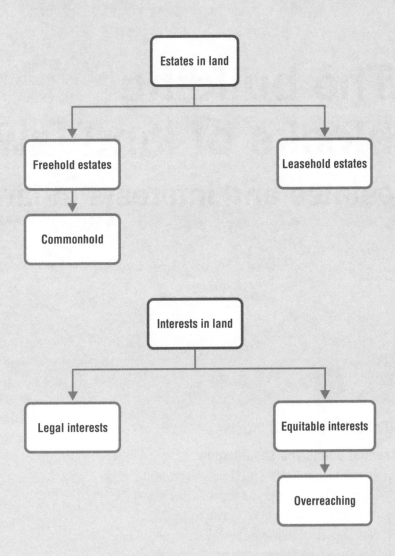

■Introduction

You must know what the fundamental terms mean and which rights can be estates and which can be interests. Registered land is also, of course, a building block of land law but you cannot progress to it unless you have mastered the fundamentals in this chapter.

This chapter and the next one (on registration of title to land) should be thought of as one: this chapter is the essential foundation and it then leads on to either registered or unregistered land.

ASSESSMENT ADVICE

An essay question will probably ask you either to:

■ Look at the distinction between legal estates and legal and equitable interests and explain their significance.

■ Look at the background to the development of land law as it is today. (This answer may require knowledge of other areas dealt with in subsequent chapters such as land registration rules (Chapter 2).)

You are less likely to get a problem question purely on the material in this chapter, as it is introductory. However, in a problem question on either unregistered or registered land you will require a sound knowledge of the material here.

■Sample question

Could you answer this question? Below is a typical essay question which could arise on this topic. Guidelines on answering this question are included at the end of this chapter while a sample problem question and guidance on tackling it can be found on the companion website.

ESSAY QUESTION

Distinguish between legal and equitable interests in land. What is the importance of the distinction?

■ What is land?

The starting point is the definition of land in s. 205(1)(ix) of the Law of Property Act (LPA) 1925. This contains the following key definitions:

KEY DEFINITION: Land

'Land ... and mines and minerals, whether or not held apart from the surface' – land is not just the actual surface but also land below and air space above. What is unsettled is how far it extends: note *Bernstein* v. *Skyviews and General Ltd* (1978) – claim by a landowner for trespass in respect of flights over his house for aerial photography rejected. The court held that a landowner only owns such airspace necessary for the reasonable enjoyment of the land.

KEY DEFINITION: Corporeal hereditaments

The land and what is attached to the land.

KEY DEFINITION: Incorporeal hereditaments

Rights over land. These include easements and profits.

When land is sold, sellers, to avoid disputes, usually provide lists of what are fixtures and fittings. See *Botham* v. *TSB Bank plc* (1996) on the distinction between fixtures and fittings.

The Treasure Act 1996 abolished the old notion of 'treasure trove' and provides that articles defined as treasure vest in the Crown.

 Make your answer stand out

There is a debate about the notion of property and thus about what are proprietary interests and you may need to discuss this in an essay question. See Gray (1991) (at 293).

EXAM TIP

In an exam essay question on the nature of property you should also refer to the change of approach brought about by the Human Rights Act 1998, below.

■ Estates in land

All land is owned by the Crown. The most that anyone can have is an estate in the land.

KEY DEFINITION: Estate in land

The rights which a person has to control and use the land. An estate owner is often called the owner of the land.

KEY DEFINITION: Freehold and Leasehold

Freehold estates last for an unlimited time and, in practice, they are perpetual, whereas leasehold estates last for a definite time.

Estates in land must be created by *deed* (see below) except in the case of leases for up to three years (s. 54(2), LPA 1925).

REVISION NOTE

Check Chapter 6 and revise the methods of creation of a lease.

KEY STATUTE

Section 1(1), LPA 1925

'The only estates in land which are capable of subsisting or of being created or conveyed at law are:

An estate in fee simple absolute in possession (legal freehold estate).

A term of years absolute (legal leasehold estate).'

Freehold estates

A freehold estate is the nearest to absolute ownership recognised by English law.

KEY DEFINITION: Fee simple absolute in possession

The terms together mean:

- **Fee**: can be inherited.
- **simple**: by anyone.
- **absolute**: will not end on a certain event, i.e. to X until he marries.
- **in possession**: not e.g. to X at 21.

It is possible to have other freehold estates (e.g. for life) but they can only exist behind a trust (see later).

All land must have a freehold owner and if the individual owner cannot be traced the ownership is held by the Crown.

Leasehold estates

Land may also be held under a leasehold estate and so there will be two estates in the same land.

KEY DEFINITION: Term of years absolute

'Term of years' means any period having a fixed and certain duration; 'absolute' appears to have no meaning beyond the fact that a term of years may be absolute even if it contains a clause enabling either party to determine it by notice.

 Make your answer stand out

You may get an essay question on the historical development of land law so consider:

- Why was the LPA 1925 passed?
- Does it need further reform?

This will be linked with the system of land registration – in particular, the LRA 2002 has updated this – see Chapter 2. For a good mark, look at Simpson (1986).

Commonhold

The concept of commonhold was introduced by the Commonhold and Leasehold Reform Act 2002, Part 1 of which, dealing with commonhold, came into force on 27 September 2004. You are less likely to get a whole question on this but an answer to an essay question on the general principles of land law will gain extra marks if you mention commonhold.

> ✓ Make your answer stand out
>
> See Smith (2004) for a discussion and analysis of commonhold.

Interests in land

KEY DEFINITION: Interest in land

A right which a person has over another's land.

Remember that an estate in land is a right which a person has over his or her land.

There are two types of interests in land:

1 Legal interests.
2 Equitable interests.

Those interests which are legal are set out below and all other interests must be equitable! Do not think about equitable interests until you have mastered legal interests.

Legal and equitable interests in land have one common feature: *they are proprietary rights in land.*

KEY DEFINITION: Proprietary rights

Capable of binding third parties, i.e. legal estates and legal and equitable interests in land, see below.

KEY DEFINITION: Personal rights

Not capable of binding third parties, e.g. licences.

Example

Z has an easement over X's land. This is an example of a proprietary right and so is capable of binding Y when X sells his land to him.

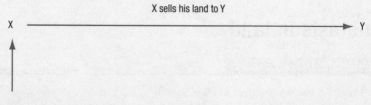

X sells his land to Y

X ⟶ Y

Z has permission from X to sit in X's garden and paint the view of the hills. This is only a licence and so it is a personal right and cannot be binding on Y.

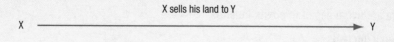

X sells his land to Y

X ⟶ Y

Legal interests in land

Note: These are defined in s. 1(2) of the LPA 1925. Only these can be legal. All interests not in this list must be equitable.

The list of interests which can be legal is:

(a) An easement, right or privilege in or over land for an interest equivalent to an estate in fee simple absolute in possession or a term of years absolute.

This includes both easements and profits à prendre.

KEY DEFINITION: Easement

Gives the right to use the land of another in some way or to prevent it from being used for certain purposes, e.g. rights of way and rights of water and light.

KEY DEFINITION: Profit

Gives the right to take something from the land of another, e.g. peat, fish, wood or grazing rights.

REVISION NOTE

You need to be absolutely clear about the distinction between these. Easements and profits are dealt with in Chapter 8.

However, to be legal the right must be held either for an indefinite time (equivalent to a fee simple) or for a definite time (equivalent to a term of years). Therefore, an easement for life or a right of drainage granted until the road is adopted by the local authority cannot be a legal interest and must be equitable.

(b) A rentcharge in possession issuing out of or charged on land being either perpetual or for a term of years absolute.

KEY DEFINITION: Rentcharge

A gives the owner the right to a periodical sum of money secured on land independently of any lease or mortgage, e.g. where the seller of land reserves an annual payment for it secured by a rentcharge. These are commonly found in the Manchester and Bristol areas.

No new rentcharges can be created after 22 July 1977 (with certain exceptions) and most rentcharges will be extinguished on 22 July 2037 or 60 years from the date of creation, whichever is the later.

(c) A charge by way of legal mortgage.

This is one of the ways of creating a legal mortgage and will be explained later in Chapter 9.

KEY DEFINITION: Mortgage

A charge on land to secure a debt.

(d) Land tax, tithe rentcharge, and any other similar charge on land which is not created by an instrument.

The common feature of any charges coming within this provision is that they are periodical payments with which land was burdened by law. The three specific charges which fell within this provision have been abolished. The part above is all that remains.

(e) Rights of entry exercisable over or in respect of a legal term of years absolute, or annexed, for any purpose, to a legal rentcharge.

A right of re-entry in a lease, if the tenant, for example, fails to pay the rent, is made an interest in land in itself. It can be attached to a legal rentcharge to secure payment of the rent.

EXAM TIP

The most common legal interests for exam purposes are in categories (a) and (c) above.

Assuming that the interest is within this list, then in order to be legal it must have been created by *deed*.

KEY STATUTE

Section 52(1), LPA 1925

Requires the use of a deed to create or convey a legal estate or interest in land.

A deed is a document which, if made before 31 July 1990, had to be sealed but this is no longer necessary.

KEY STATUTE

Section 1(2) and (3) Law of Property (Miscellaneous Provisions) Act 1989

An instrument shall not be a deed unless:

■ it makes clear that it is intended to be a deed;

■ it is signed by the person executing it and by a witness present at the same time who also signs it;

■ it is delivered by the person executing it or by someone on his behalf.

Example one

X agrees with Y by a deed that Y can have a right of way across X's land for the rest of Y's life.

Step one: Identify the right – an easement.

Step two: Is it legal or equitable? As it is for life it can only be equitable, even if it is in a deed.

Example two

X agrees with Y that Y can have a right of way across X's land.

Step one: Identify the right – an easement.

Step two: Is it legal or equitable? As it does not say that the easement is only for Y's life, we can assume that it is for ever. So it can be legal or equitable.

Step three: Is it in a deed? Yes, so it is legal.

Note: Sometimes the interest is not actually granted by deed but is implied into it. See Chapter 8 for examples.

Equitable interests in land

All other interests in land are equitable.

KEY DEFINITION: Equitable

This term means that the right was originally only recognised by the Court of Chancery, which dealt with equitable rights, and not by the Courts of Common Law.

You do not need to know equity in detail in order to pass exams in land law, but you should keep this fundamental characteristic of equity in mind:

Equity often applied where the application of the strict rules of the common law would not have produced a just result. The effect was that equity often did not insist on the observance of formalities, such as the need for a right to be granted in a deed (above). You can find out more about equity in the companion book to this one: *Law Express: Equity and Trusts*.

> ❗ Don't be tempted to...
>
> Make sure that you revise the rules for deciding whether an interest is equitable or not. In land law exams you should ask two questions to decide if the right is equitable:
>
> ■ Is it in the above list of legal interests? If not, then it must be equitable.
>
> ■ If it is in the above list, then was it created by deed? If not, then it must be equitable.

REVISION NOTE

Chapter 2 also deals with another way in which a right can become equitable rather than legal: if it is not registered as required by the LRA 2002. Keep this point at the back of your mind for now, but do not worry about registered land yet.

Interests under trusts

KEY DEFINITION: Trust

Arises when property is held by one person (the trustee) on trust for another (the beneficiary).

X (trustee) ⸺⸺⸺⸺⸺⸺⸺⸺⸺⸺⸺⸺⸺⸺→ Y (beneficiary)

X is the legal owner but Y has the equitable interest.

REVISION NOTE

Many trusts met in land law exams are not created by the parties specifically agreeing to set up a trust but in other ways, e.g. by one party (Y) paying part of the purchase price of property which is actually held in X's name. Here equity implies a trust in favour of Y. This topic is dealt with in full in Chapter 4 but you must remember this example now as it will often appear in this chapter and the next one.

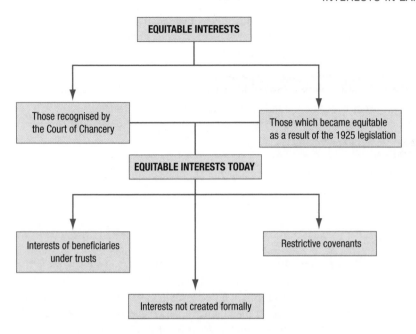

Therefore, the legal ownership and the benefit are split and the common law, apparently because it could not cope with the idea of splitting these two, refused to recognise trusts and allowed the trustee to ignore the rights of the *beneficiaries*. Equity, however, enforced trusts because this was a matter of conscience, i.e. the trustee had never been intended to have complete control of the property. You will find later that a trustee can also be a beneficiary if this was intended.

REVISION NOTE

A common example of a trust is where a person (X) contributes to the purchase of land but the legal title is held in the name of Y. Y will hold the land on trust for X in the absence of a contrary intention. See Chapters 2, 3 and 4 and the *Tizard* case (Chapter 2). Keep this example of a trust in mind: it is frequently met in land law.

Interests not created formally

If a contract has been made to create an interest in land then equity may, at its discretion, enforce it by a decree of specific performance or restrain its breach by an injunction. This is in accordance with the equitable maxim that 'equity looks on that as done which ought to be done'. This means that when a deed is required to create an estate or interest in land and there is no deed, equity may still regard the interest subsisting in land as an equitable interest.

KEY DEFINITION: Specific performance

A court order which commands the performance of a contract.

KEY DEFINITION: Injunction

A court order which either orders a lawful act to be done or restrains an unlawful act.

Example

X agrees to grant Y a right of way over his land. This is not in a deed. As in the above examples, we can assume that it is to last for ever, as it does not say that it is for life. However, the lack of a deed would still be fatal to it being a legal easement. However, equity may come to the rescue and declare it to be an equitable easement. Another example is an agreement for a lease. See *Walsh* v. *Lonsdale* in Chapter 6.

EXAM TIP

How to tell if there is a deed or just an agreement:

■ The word 'grants' usually indicates a deed as this is the idea behind one: the right of way is granted by X to Y and not agreed by them.

■ The words 'agrees to grant' indicates just an agreement as it points to the future and this fits with the idea behind equity: it enforces a contract to grant an interest in the future.

KEY STATUTE

Section 2 Law of Property (Miscellaneous Provisions) Act 1989

Contracts for the sale or other disposition of an interest in land made on or after 27 September 1989 must:

■ be in writing;

■ contain all the terms agreed by the parties; and

■ be signed by all the parties.

Therefore, equity will enforce a contract for, for example, an equitable easement provided that it satisfies these requirements. Contracts made before that date do not require writing and there are several fairly recent cases in which this point has been important. Another example of an equitable interest in this connection is an estate contract, which is a contract to convey a legal estate.

Note the effect of electronic conveyancing on the formalities required for deeds and contracts set out above.

Section 91 of the LRA 2002 provides that, in order to pave the way for the introduction of electronic conveyancing (see Chapter 2), electronic documents will be capable of satisfying these requirements but the details have not all been worked out.

Restrictive covenants

KEY DEFINITION: Restrictive covenant

Where a person covenants in a deed not to use his land in a certain way or to do something on his land, e.g. to keep fences in repair or not to build on the land. See Chapter 7.

These have only ever been enforced in equity.

REVISION NOTE

Rights created by equitable estoppel may also be regarded as equitable interests. See Chapter 5.

Why do you need to know the distinction between legal and equitable interests?

Because of the different effect which they have on a purchaser of the land.

REVISION NOTE

When you read Chapter 2, you will see the significance of the distinction between legal and equitable interests.

Note that if a person is not the purchaser, then that person takes the land with all equitable rights.

EXAM TIP

Check in a question whether a person, for instance, inherited the land. If so, he or she will not be a purchaser.

◼ Overreaching

KEY DEFINITION: Overreaching

The process by which equitable rights which exist under a trust of land are removed from the land and transferred to the money (called capital money) which has been paid to purchase the land. The effect is to give the purchaser automatic priority over equitable interests under a trust.

KEY STATUTE

Section 2(1), LPA 1925

'A conveyance to a purchaser of a legal estate in land shall overreach any equitable interest or power affecting the estate, whether he has notice thereof ...' There are various instances where overreaching can take place but the relevant one here is

Section 2(1)(ii): where the provisions of s. 27 of the LPA regarding the payment of capital money are complied with, i.e. the capital money is paid to at least two trustees or a trust corporation.

Note carefully this vital restriction on overreaching: it can only take place if the transaction is made by at least two trustees or a trust corporation.

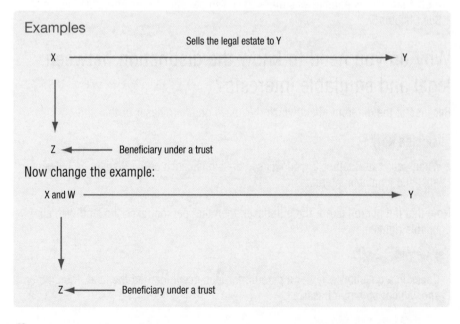

Examples

X ——— Sells the legal estate to Y ———→ Y

Z ←——— Beneficiary under a trust

Now change the example:

X and W ——————————————→ Y

Z ←——— Beneficiary under a trust

Here Y will not be bound by Z's interest as the transaction was entered into by two trustees (X and W) and so Z's interest in the property is overreached and is transferred to the proceeds of sale. The effect is that Y need not concern himself about them but Z may claim against X and W for any share of the proceeds of sale which she feels belongs to her.

EXAM TIP

If you get a problem question on the lines of the facts in *Kingsnorth Finance Co. Ltd* v. *Tizard* (1986) (i.e. rights of beneficiaries under a trust of land, see Chapter 2) check first how many persons are transferring the legal estate. If it is one, there cannot be overreaching. More than one, and overreaching will take place.

KEY CASE

City of London Building Society v. *Flegg* [1987] 3 All ER 435 (HL)
Concerning: overreaching the beneficial interests in a trust of land

Facts

Mr and Mrs MB were the registered proprietors of a house but over half the purchase price had been raised by Mr and Mrs F, the parents of Mrs MB, who were also to live at the house. Accordingly, the house was held on trust for all four of them. Mr and Mrs MB then, without the knowledge of Mrs MB's parents, raised two further charges over the property and then defaulted on the repayments. The lender sought possession and it was held that the interests of the parents had been overreached by the charges and that their rights now only existed in the proceeds of sale.

Legal principle

The interests of beneficiaries in a trust of land are overreached if the transaction is entered into by two or more trustees.

Note that under s. 205(1)(xxi) of the LPA a purchase includes a chargee by way of legal mortgage, i.e., in practice, a lender under a mortgage.

Make your answer stand out

In *State Bank of India* v. *Sood* (1997) it was held that overreaching applies not only where capital money is actually paid but also where the mortgage was created as security for existing and future liabilities. Thus, at the time, no capital money (i.e. mortgage finance here) changed hands.

■ Land law and the Human Rights Act (HRA) 1998

This can be relevant to a land law exam in two ways:

1 as a separate essay question;
2 to mention when you are looking at a specific area, e.g. adverse possession. You can boost your marks here by mentioning this Act.

Think of this quote from Mummery LJ in the CA in *Newham LBC* v. *Kibata* (2003), who considered that the HRA has 'brought about a new species of property right in the home'. At a wider level the debate is about the place, not only of land law, but of law itself, in society.

Look at the following cases (also remember to keep up to date on this area as it is moving quickly!).

Harrow LBC v. *Qazi* (2004)
Connors v. *United Kingdom* (2005)
Doherty v. *Birmingham City Council* (2006)
McCann v. *United Kingdom* (2008)

Note the striking contrast between the approaches of the HL in *Qazi* and the ECtHR in *Connors*, as well as the decisions of the HL in *Kay* v. *Lambeth LBC* and *Leeds CC* v. *Price* (2006), where the majority, in effect, reaffirmed *Qazi*.

 Make your answer stand out

English common law has historically emphasised possession of land rather than ownership. Indeed, as explained above, no one can actually own land. Emphasis on possession is still true today, e.g. a person will not have a leasehold estate unless he or she is granted exclusive possession of the leasehold property – see Chapter 6.

The common law's emphasis on possession as the basis of title is now giving way to a state-regulated system based on land registration. See Gray and Gray (2003), where the authors speak of a norm of 'rationality' in respect of sales and mortgages of land.

REVISION NOTE

What is meant by possession? See the requirements for adverse possession in Chapter 10.

Distinguish possession from occupation – an occupier may or may not have both possession and a legal estate in the land. A personal occupier who does not have exclusive possession will have just a licence (see Chapter 6); however, an occupier with a proprietary (not just personal) interest in the land may have a right which binds those who acquire the land – see Chapter 2.

■ **Chapter summary**: putting it all together

Test yourself

- ☐ Can you tick all the points from the **revision checklist** at the beginning of this chapter?
- ☐ Attempt the **sample question** from the beginning of this chapter using the answer guidelines below.
- ☐ Go to the **companion website** to access more revision support online, including interactive quizzes, sample questions with answer guidelines, 'You be the marker' exercises, flashcards and podcasts you can download.

Answer guidelines

See the essay question at the start of this chapter.

Approaching the question

This question should be relatively straightforward as it just requires you to recognise legal and equitable interests in land and distinguish between them.

Important points to include

■ Begin by giving a clear explanation of what these terms mean, avoiding too much elaboration – never neglect basic points!

■ Then go through the main examples of each, aiming above all here for accuracy because you will need to apply these rules in more complex situations later and you must get these 'building blocks' right.

■ Then explain the importance of the distinction, i.e. the effect on third-party rights. Again, clear and accurate explanations please!

 Make your answer stand out

At this stage an answer will stand out if it just shows a clear grasp of the issues and, if possible, an exploration of the case law on the meaning of 'notice' in connection with equitable interests (see Chapter 2).

READ TO IMPRESS

Bright, 'Of estates and interests: a tale of ownership and property rights', in Bright and Dewar (eds), *Land Law, Themes and Perspectives*, Oxford University Press, Oxford (1998).

Gray, 'Property in thin air' (1991), 50 CLJ 252.

Gray, 'Land law and human rights', in Tee (ed.), *Land Law, Issues, Debates, Policy*, Willan, Uffculme (2004).

Gray and Gray, 'The rhetoric of realty', in Getzler (ed.), *Rationalising Property: Equity and Trusts*, Butterworths, London (2003) especially p. 206.

Lewis, 'The European ceiling on human rights' [2007] PL 720.

Simpson, *A History of the Land Law*, 2nd edn, Oxford University Press, Oxford (1986), especially pp. 242–92, chapters X and XI.

Smith, 'The purity of commonholds' [2004] Conv 194.

NOTES

NOTES

Registered and unregistered title to land

2

Revision checklist

Essential points you should know:

- [ ] What is meant by registration of titles to land and how this differs from unregistered title to land
- [ ] Which dispositions must be completed by registration
- [ ] What is meant by the term 'interests which can override'
- [ ] What is meant by the term 'protected registered interests' and how such interests can be protected
- [ ] Which rights must be registered as land charges to bind a purchaser
- [ ] Whether purchasers are bound by legal interests and equitable interests which are not registrable as land charges

■ Topic map

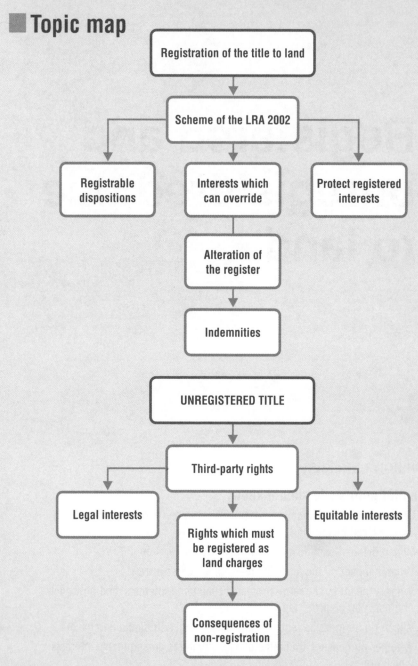

A printable version of this topic map is available from **www.pearsoned.co.uk/lawexpress**

■Introduction

This is the indispensable topic of land law. Whether title to land is registered or not will come into virtually all problem questions:

- Adverse possession.
- Leases.
- Licences and estoppel.
- Easements and profits.
- Freehold covenants.
- Mortgages.

It can also form the subject of an essay question. We will first look at the position where title is registered and then at when it is unregistered.

ASSESSMENT ADVICE

Essay questions Obvious areas for essay questions are:

- The LRA 2002: how has it changed the system of registered land and how far has it been successful?
- The existence of overriding interests: should they still exist?
- A comparison between the systems of registered and unregistered land.

Problem questions Problem questions may link with other areas or be self-contained. An obvious area to link to is trusts of the home (Chapter 4), where you could be required to decide whether a party has an equitable interest and then to decide whether it is overriding.

■Sample question

Could you answer this question? Below is a typical problem question which could arise on this topic. Guidelines on answering this question are included at the end of this chapter while a sample essay question and guidance on tackling it can be found on the companion website.

PROBLEM QUESTION

John has bought a freehold house with some farmland from Steve.

After John's purchase, Fred, Susie and Jean, who are all neighbours, come to see him with letters signed by Steve.

Fred has a letter granting him the right to cut wood from trees on the land.

Susie has a letter agreeing to grant her a lease of one acre of the farmland. Susie has not started to use the land.

Jean has a letter stating that she has a licence to park her caravan on the land.

In addition, Elsie, Steve's mother arrives and says that she paid half the purchase price when Steve bought the house and so she has a right to stay there. Elsie was away on holiday when John purchased the house.

Advise John on whether he is bound by any of these claims. How would your answer differ if title was unregistered?

■ Principles of land registration

An essay question in an exam may ask you to explain the principles of land registration. You need to emphasise that the Land Registration Act 1925 (LRA) (now the LRA 2002) provided for a system of registration of titles and not title to land. Therefore, there may be more then one title applicable to the same piece of land. The vital difference from the unregistered system, which is dealt with later in this chapter, is that here title to land is registered rather than just charges against the estate owner.

The intention is that all land shall be held under registered title as soon as practicable.

The other main aim of the LRA 2002 is to make arrangements to the legislation to enable dispositions of registered land to be dealt with electronically. It is most unlikely that you will need to discuss this in detail.

The land registration scheme rests on three principles:

- Mirror Principle – all facts relevant to the title are to be found on the register.
- Curtain Principle – purchasers need not look beyond the register and are not concerned with trusts.
- Insurance Principle – any flaw in the register leads to the payment of compensation to a person affected.

■Scheme of the Land Registration Act

The LRA 2002 takes the different types of estates and interests in land (see Chapter 1) and classifies them for the purposes of land registration in the following ways:

- Dispositions which must be completed by registration.

- Unregistered dispositions which override registered dispositions. These correspond to the old category of overriding interests and the effect is that a buyer of the land can be bound by an interest that is not on the register. This is a highly significant area and often forms the subject of examination questions. We shall continue to refer to these as overriding interests.

- Interests which must be protected by an entry against the title which they bind. These were formerly known as *minor interests* and this term will continue to be used.

These categories will be explored in detail later but it is absolutely essential that you both know them and can apply them in an exam.

> **EXAM TIP**
>
> A through knowledge of the three ways in which the LRA 2002 classifies estates and interests in land will gain you marks in virtually all problem questions in the exam, not just questions specifically on land registration.

■Registrable dispositions

> **KEY STATUTE**
>
> ### Section 27(1), LRA 2002
>
> If a disposition is required to be completed by registration, then it does not operate at law until it is registered in accordance with the requirements.

> **KEY DEFINITION: Registrable disposition**
>
> One that must be completed by registration.

The dispositions which must be completed by registration are set out in s. 27 of the LRA:

- **Transfer of the registered freehold estate**. This includes transfers by any of the following methods:
  (a) for valuable or other consideration;

(b) by way of gift;

(c) in pursuance of a court order;

(d) transfer by personal representatives on death.

- **The grant of a legal lease with more than seven years to run**. In addition, certain leases for less than seven years are registrable, e.g. those which take effect more than three months after the date of the grant.

- **Certain other leases and rights arising under leases**, e.g. registration of the grant of a right to buy a lease under the Housing Act 1985.

- **The express grant or reservation of legal easements, legal profits, legal rentcharges.**

- **A first legal mortgage created out of the estate**. This will apply whenever existing legal mortgages are discharged and a new mortgage created. This rule has proved to be one of the main means of transferring land from the unregistered system to the registered system.

The above are the 'triggers' to registration of title. They cover almost all the possibilities but not quite: the appointment of new trustees and registration of the freehold on the grant of a long lease are not triggers.

! Don't be tempted to...

Be sure that you understand the *relationship* between s. 28 and s. 29 of the LRA 2002.

KEY STATUTE

Section 28, LRA 2002

This sets out the basic rule: the priority of an interest affecting a registered estate or charge is not affected by a disposition of the estate or charge. The effect is that priority of interests in registered land depends on their date of creation.

Before you try to make sense of this, turn to:

KEY STATUTE

Section 29, LRA 2002

This section provides (not the exact words) that the effect of a registered disposition made for *valuable consideration* (my italics) is that it takes priority over any rights affecting the estate prior to the disposition which are not protected by registration or are overriding. Thus, an interest which is neither overriding nor protected by an entry on the register will not be binding on the purchaser.

The relationship between ss. 28 and 29 can be seen in this example.

Example

John, the registered proprietor of Blackacre, has made a contract to sell it to Mary.

(a) John dies and Anne inherits Blackacre. Mary's contract binds Anne as Mary's right was created first. This is s. 28.
(b) John sells Blackacre to Anne. As the disposition was for valuable consideration (the word 'sells' indicates this), s. 29 applies and, if Mary's contract was not protected by registration, it will not bind Anne.

The relationship between s. 28 and s. 29 was considered in *Halifax plc.* v. *Curry Popeck* (2008), where the issue was the priority of two mortgages to different lenders over a property. The property had been transferred fraudulently and therefore no question of valuable consideration arose, so s. 28 applied. Thus the mortgage created first had priority. The reason for the litigation was that the first lender had not acquired an immediate charge over the property as there was no contract to satisfy s. 2 of the Law of Property (Miscellaneous Provisions) Act 1989. However, the first lender did have a right by proprietary estoppel.

REVISION NOTE

Go back to Chapter 1 and revise s. 2 of the Law of Property (Miscellaneous Provisions) Act 1989 and check Chapter 5 for proprietary estoppel.

REVISION NOTE

Section 28 can apply in a problem involving adverse possession – see Chapter 10 – as well, of course, in other areas, so check whether a person has acquired the land by gift (which includes inheritance). If it was acquired by sale, s. 29 applies.

The net effect of all this is that the basic rule in s. 28 is an exception and usually s. 29 applies as the land will have been sold and not given away.

There are few dispositions of freehold land or leases with at least seven years which will not be caught by the above rules and which will not need to be registered. One example is an assignment of a mortgage.

Voluntary registration is also possible, e.g. a freehold estate may be registered even though it is not being transferred.

> **EXAM TIP**
>
> When revising, remember ss. 27, 28 and 29 – these are all vital sections of the LRA 2002.

Overriding interests

> **EXAM TIP**
>
> This is probably the most common topic on registered land for both essay questions and problem questions.

> **KEY DEFINITION: Overriding interest**
>
> An unregistered disposition which overrides a registered disposition.

The LRA 2002 distinguishes between:

- Interests which override on first registration of the land; and
- Interests which override on subsequent registration of the land.

Why?

This is because the effect of a first and a subsequent registration is different:

Example one

John sells 112 High Street, which has unregistered title, to Mary. Following the sale, Mary registers the title. John's son Christopher, who contributed to the purchase price when John bought the house, still lives there. Christopher may have an equitable interest in the property. It is not at this time an overriding interest as title to 112 High Street has not been registered. The time for deciding if Christopher's interest is binding on Mary is when Mary acquired the title to it and the principles of unregistered land are relevant – see below. However, when Mary's title is registered later, Christopher's interest may then count as an overriding interest.

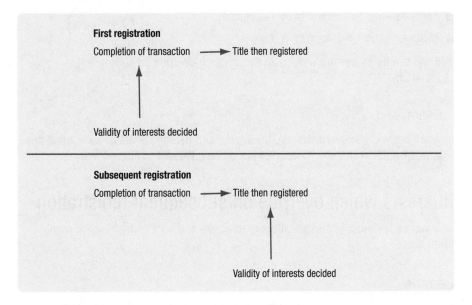

First registration

Completion of transaction ⟶ Title then registered

Validity of interests decided

Subsequent registration

Completion of transaction ⟶ Title then registered

Validity of interests decided

Example two

Now the title is registered. This time the crucial time is when Mary's title is registered. Now Christopher's interest counts as an overriding interest throughout the transaction.

 Make your answer stand out

See Law Commission Paper 271 (2001), especially para. 8.3.

EXAM TIP

If a problem question says that the title to land *is* registered and then asks you about, e.g., the effect on third-party rights of a sale, that sale will result in a subsequent registration.

Interests which override on first registration

- Legal leases not exceeding seven years.
- Interests of persons in actual occupation.

- Legal easements and profits (not equitable).
- Miscellaneous – e.g. local land charges.

You will see that these are wider than those which override on subsequent registration.

> ### Example
>
> When there is a first registration, the interests of persons in actual occupation are binding whether or not the occupier has made enquiries of them.

Interests which override on subsequent registration

This will be the most important category in exams and so it is dealt with in much more detail.

Leases

- Legal leases with more than seven years to run are registrable dispositions.
- Legal leases not exceeding seven years are overriding interests. (Sch. 3, para. 1)
- Equitable leases should be protected by registration as minor interests (estate contracts); but if they are not and if the leaseholder is in actual occupation, then they may have an overriding interest under Sch. 3, para. 2, LRA 2002, below.

Note: s. 118(1) of the LRA 2002 gives the Lord Chancellor the power to reduce the period for which registration of a legal lease is required. It is likely to be reduced to three years.

Overriding interests of occupiers

KEY STATUTE

Schedule 3, para. 2, LRA 2002

An interest belonging at the time of the disposition to a person in actual occupation except for:

(i) an interest of a person of whom enquiry was made before the disposition and who failed to disclose the right when he could have been reasonably expected to do so;
(ii) an interest which belongs to a person whose occupation would not have been obvious on a reasonable inspection of the land at the time of the disposition and of which the person to whom the disposition was made does not have actual knowledge.

This area will come up somewhere in your exam either as:

- a direct question on land registration; or, for example:
- in a question on adverse possession; or
- in a question on leases.

✓ Make your answer stand out

The law changed from the LRA 1925 when the corresponding provision (s. 70(1)(g), LRA 1925) did not provide that an overriding interest could be lost in Sch. 3, para. 2 case (ii) above. The new provision has in effect introduced the idea of notice found in unregistered land to registered land. This is controversial. See the further reading, below, for pointers on where to research this.

REVISION NOTE

See *Kingsnorth Finance Co. Ltd* v. *Tizard* and compare the solution there with that in Sch. 3, para. 2 above.

In a typical question based on *Williams & Glyn's Bank* v. *Boland* (below) you should approach a problem question in this way:

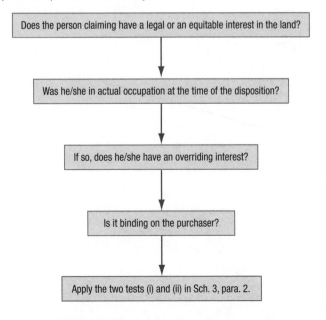

Does the person claiming have a legal or an equitable interest in the land?

↓

Was he/she in actual occupation at the time of the disposition?

↓

If so, does he/she have an overriding interest?

↓

Is it binding on the purchaser?

↓

Apply the two tests (i) and (ii) in Sch. 3, para. 2.

The cases decided under the LRA 1925 are still of use and establish the following principles:

- When does a right qualify as for overriding status? *National Provincial Bank* v. *Ainsworth* (1965): when it is a proprietary interest in land, whether it is legal or equitable. This principle is given statutory force by s. 29(1) of the LRA 2002 (see above) which refers to any interest '*affecting the estate*', i.e. a proprietary interest.

KEY CASE

Williams & Glyn's Bank v. *Boland* [1980] 2 All ER 408 (HL)

Concerning: occupation of spouse giving an overriding interest

Facts

The wife had contributed to the purchase price of property and so had acquired a beneficial interest in it. The husband mortgaged it to the bank which sought possession when he did not keep up the repayments.

Legal principle

As the wife was in occupation under an equitable interest (i.e. a proprietary interest), she had an overriding interest which bound the bank.

The situation in this case and other similar ones can be seen in this way and you may find it useful to make a similar diagram when you get a problem question on this area:

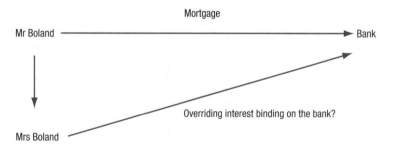

Equitable interest? If so, is she also in occupation?

EXAM TIP

A problem question may ask you to discuss in more detail whether a person in Mrs Boland's position does have an equitable interest.

Check Chapter 4 and make sure that you are clear on the principles in *Stack* v. *Dowden*.

■ Can occupation be lost by temporary absence? See *Chhoakar* v. *Chhoakar* (1984).

 Make your answer stand out

This is a common area for exam questions and the underlying principle is that of symbolic occupation. What if the claimant was away on a round-the-world trip which was to take two years? Note *Stockholm Finance Ltd* v. *Garden Holdings Inc.* (1995) and also *Kling* v. *Keston Properties Ltd* (1985) – occupation of a garage shown by the presence of a car in it.

KEY CASE

Abbey National Building Society v. *Cann* [1990] 1 All ER 1085 (HL)
Concerning: time at which an overriding interest under Sch. 3, para. 2 takes effect

Facts

Carpets were laid out and furniture moved before completion without the consent of the seller.

Legal principle

In order to bind a purchaser, there must be occupation at the time of the disposition, i.e. completion of the purchase, and here there were only acts preparatory to completion. In addition, where title is registered, the rights must remain subsisting at the time of registration.

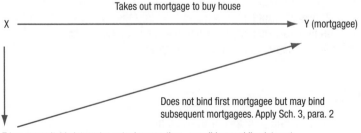

Takes out mortgage to buy house

X ──────────────────────────────→ Y (mortgagee)

Does not bind first mortgagee but may bind
subsequent mortgagees. Apply Sch. 3, para. 2

Z has an equitable interest + actual occupation = possible overriding interest

Make your answer stand out

The decision in *Cann* denied that there is a *scintilla temporis* (fragment of time) between:

(a) completion of the purchase;
(b) creation of the mortgage.

The argument was that a beneficial interest could arise between (a) and (b) and so could bind the mortgagee. This was rejected.

 Make your answer stand out

The effect of this decision was to confine the principle in *Boland* to subsequent mortgages and was considered part of 'the retreat from *Boland*'. Other cases which are said to be examples of this are:

- *City of London Building Society* v. *Flegg* (1987): an overriding interest can be overreached.

- *Paddington Building Society* v. *Mendelsohn* (1985): occupier may have consented by implication to the mortgage; the principle in this case can often be applied alongside that in *Cann* (above) in an exam.

- *Equity and Law Home Loans Ltd* v. *Prestidge* (1992): a person who consents to a mortgage is deemed to consent to a later mortgage which replaces it to the extent of the amount secured by the first mortgage plus interest. This applies even if the person did not know of the replacement mortgage.

- *Hypo Mortgage Services Ltd* v. *Robinson* (1997): a child cannot be in actual occupation. The reason is that otherwise the interests of lenders on mortgages could be defeated by conferring a (possibly very small) interest on a minor.

- *Ferrishurst Ltd* v. *Wallcite Ltd* (1999): an occupier need not be in occupation of the whole of the registered plot but this was reversed by Sch. 3, para. 2, LRA which provides that an overriding interest only extends to land of which a person is in actual occupation. Mention this in an essay: example of a reduction in the scope of overriding interests.

REVISION NOTE

Check Chapter 1 for the principle of overreaching.

In an essay question where you are discussing the position of lenders you could make a link with the law on undue influence. As explained in Chapter 9, in *Royal Bank of Scotland plc* v. *Etridge (No. 2)* (2001), the HL decided that provided that a lender follows certain steps then the loan made will not be affected by the undue influence of another. Thus, here also there is greater protection for lenders than before.

See *Bank of Baroda* v. *Dhillon* (1998) in Chapter 3. If a mortgagee applies for a sale under s. 14(1) of the Trusts of Land and Appointment of Trustees Act 1996 (TLATA) rather than under the mortgagee's own power of sale, this will in effect override an overriding interest. It may be, though, as in this case, that the occupier, as a beneficiary under a trust, will be entitled to first payment out of the proceeds of sale. This could be a neat way to round off an answer to a problem question.

Easements and profits

- Legal easements and profits created expressly on or after 13 October 2003 (i.e. by deed) are registrable dispositions.

- Equitable easements and profits created on or after 13 October 2003 can now only take effect as minor interests.

- The only new legal easements and profits that can be overriding are those:
  - created by implied reservation;
  - created by implied grant (rule in *Wheeldon* v. *Burrows* (1879) or s. 62(1), LPA 1925);
  - created by prescription (Sch. 3, para. 3, LRA 2002).

Where an easement can be overriding then it will be in exactly the same way as for rights of occupiers (see Sch. 3, para. 2, above) but there is one extra point to remember:

Where the person entitled to the easement or profit proves that it has been exercised in the year previous to the disposition then it will in effect always be overriding.

Example

X has a right of way (easement) over Y's land. Y sells the land to Z.

- If the easement was granted by deed, it will not bind Z unless registered.
- If the easement was granted by agreement but not in a deed, it is equitable and will not bind Z unless protected on the register as a minor interest.
- If the easement was created by implied grant or prescription, it can be overriding but will not bind Z where cases (i) or (ii) in Sch. 3, para. 2 (above) apply. However, it will bind Z if X exercised it in the year previous to the disposition (sale to Z).

REVISION NOTE

Check Chapter 1 and make sure that you know the rules on creation of an equitable interest by agreement.

Local land charges

You will not get a detailed question on these in the exam but you should know what they are. They are not the same as land charges in unregistered land – see below) and are contained in a register maintained by district (or unitary) councils, e.g. compulsory purchase orders, tree preservation orders.

 Make your answer stand out

This whole area, and particularly overriding interests, is a very likely one for an essay question. Look at the further reading listed at the end of this chapter.

Transitional provisions

- Legal leases which were overriding before 13 October 2003 (i.e. legal leases granted for up to 21 years) remain so.
- Legal and equitable easements and profits which were overriding before 13 October 2003 remain so.
- Interests which cease to be overriding in 2013, e.g. franchise (right to hold a market) and liability to repair the chancel of a church. Until then they bind on first and subsequent registrations.

See *Aston Cantlow PCC* v. *Wallbank* (2003), where the HL rejected a claim that such liability was in breach of the Human Rights Act 1998. The Parochial Church Council was not a public authority and, in any event, although it did amount to an interference with property, the existence of such an overriding interest was not incompatible with the ECHR.

REVISION NOTE

Check Chapter 1 for details of the effect of the ECHR on land law.

Overriding interests which are abolished, i.e. do not override under either first or subsequent registration:

■ Rights acquired or in the course of acquisition under the Limitation Acts – because of new rules for acquiring title here.

REVISION NOTE

Check Chapter 10 and make sure that you understand and can apply the rules on acquisition of title by adverse possession.

■ Equitable easements.

Make your answer stand out

The existence of overriding interests has been criticised and you should be prepared for an essay question asking you whether they can be justified. The following reasons are put forward to justify their continued existence. Look at them and then read further to expand these points.

■ They can easily be discovered by a purchaser.
■ The value which is protected by the overriding interest is greater than the value of having all interests registered.
■ It is not worth putting some interests on the register.

■ Protected registered interests: minor interests

These were formerly known as minor interests and this term will continue to be used here.

KEY DEFINITION: Protected registered interests

Interests in land which are not overriding and include: restrictive covenants, equitable easements and profits, estate contracts and rights of beneficiaries under a trust.

Most of these must be protected by an entry on the register to bind a purchaser. Note one significant change from the pre-LRA 2002 law: where an overriding interest is protected on the register by a notice, it ceases to be an overriding interest even if the notice is later removed from the register (s. 29(3), LRA). There are two ways in which an interest can be protected:

- **By a notice**. This can either be entered with the consent of the registered proprietor (RP) or unilaterally. If it is the latter, the RP can object and the Registrar decides the validity of the claim. Entry on the register does not mean that the interest is recognised by the law as valid; it simply means that it has priority over other interests (s. 32(3) LRA 2002). Certain interests cannot be protected by the entry of a notice: e.g. leases for less than three years and interests under a trust of land (s. 33 LRA 2002).

! Don't be tempted to...

Be sure that you check the possibility that a right may be *both* a minor interest and an overriding interest.

Example

An equitable lease is a minor interest, but if the lessee is in actual occupation, he or she may have an overriding interest.

Example

John agrees with Jane that she shall have a lease of Blackacre. This is an equitable lease and is a minor interest. Jane then goes into occupation under the lease. She now has an overriding interest as a person in actual occupation.

REVISION NOTE

See Chapter 3 to revise joint tenancies and tenancies in common, and Chapter 6 for equitable leases.

■ **By a restriction.** Section 44(1) of the LRA provides that where two or more persons are registered as proprietors, a restriction must be entered to ensure that interests capable of being overreached, in fact, are overreached. This applies where the beneficial interest is held under a tenancy in common as the beneficial interest is held in separate shares, but not where it is held under a joint tenancy where the beneficial interest will vest in the surviving joint tenant.

 Make your answer stand out

Law Commission Paper 254 envisages the possibility that the courts will still have power to set aside a disposition procured by fraud (see para. 3.49). It will be interesting to see whether and, if so how, this power is exercised.

REVISION NOTE

The LRA also deals with the law on adverse possession, which is considered in Chapter 10.

■ Alteration of the register

This is unlikely to appear as a major issue in the exam, but you could mention it in an essay question on how the land registration system works. The rules on when the register can be altered are in s. 65 and Sch. 4, LRA 2002.

■ Indemnities

The principle is that, if it turns out that the register needs to be altered, compensation can be paid to whoever has suffered loss. The details are in s. 103 and Sch. 8, LRA 2002.

 Make your answer stand out

There is a tendency, since the LRA 2002 came into force, to restrict the creation of legal rights off the register. Thus the law on adverse possession (see Chapter 10) has changed to make acquisition of rights by this method much more difficult and the Law Commission's Consultation Paper 186 (see Chapter 8) suggests restrictions on the creation of easements by implied grant and prescription. A good point to boost your mark, especially in essays.

◼ Unregistered title to land

Meaning of 'unregistered title to land'

This term simply means that the title to the land itself has not been registered, unlike in registered land. Therefore, when buying and selling the land, it is necessary to rely on an examination of the title deeds to the property and make other enquiries rather than having the register to rely on.

However, this does not mean that there is no system of registration at all. Instead, some rights must be registered as land charges but, as the actual title to the land is not registered, they are registered against the name of the estate owner, i.e. the owner of the legal estate of freehold or leasehold.

Do check that you understand this point and, above all, do not confuse registration of land charges with land registration itself.

◼ Rights which must be registered as land charges

There are two crucial points about the land charges scheme which you must remember for your exam:

- A registered land charge is automatically binding on a purchaser: the fact that a purchaser has no notice of it is irrelevant. The purchaser is expected to check the land charges register.

- If a land charge is not registered, it will not be binding on a purchaser, even if he/she does have notice.

To sum up: the only thing that matters is whether the right was registered as a land charge.

What rights must be registered as land charges?

Under the Land Charges Act 1925 (now the Land Charges Act 1972) a system was introduced under which the rights registrable as land charges are classified under the headings of A, B, C, D, E and F. They are set out in s. 2 of the 1972 Act.

The ones to remember for the exam are:

Class C(i): puisne mortgage – i.e. a second or subsequent mortgage. These are legal mortgages which are not protected by the deposit of the title deeds to the property as the first mortgagee will have these. These are the only legal interests which are registrable as land charges.

Class C(iv): an estate contract. These include contracts to buy the fee simple and contracts for a lease – equitable leases – see Chapter 6.

Class D(ii): a restrictive covenant entered into on or after 1 January 1926.

Class D(iii): an equitable easement created or arising on or after 1 January 1926.

You should learn the parts in italics very carefully.

In addition, the exam may require a knowledge of a *Class F Land Charge*. Under the Family Law Act 1996, spouses and (since the Civil Partnerships Act 2004) civil partners have a personal right of occupation of the family home and this can be enforced against a purchaser if registered. Note that this is a personal right and does not give the spouse or civil partner an interest in the land.

■ Consequences of non-registration

KEY STATUTE

Section 4, Land Charges Act 1972

Land charges in categories C(i), and F are void against a purchaser of any interests in the land (s. 4(5)).

Land charges in the other categories C(iv), D(ii) and D(iii) are void only against a purchaser for money or money's worth (s. 4(6)).

KEY STATUTE

Section 199(1)(i), LPA 1925

If a right is capable of registration as a land charge but is not so registered, then a purchaser is not prejudicially affected by notice of it. The effect is that a purchaser is not bound by it.

See *Midland Bank Trust Co. Ltd* v. *Green* (1981) for an illustration of this principle and contrast *Lloyds Bank* v. *Carrick* (1996), where, although an estate contract was not registered as a land charge, it could still bind a purchaser as the contract created a trust or, alternatively, an estoppel.

our answer stand out

exam marks by reading the judgment of Lord Wilberforce in the HL
ank Trust Co. Ltd v. Green (1981) and contrasting the approach of
R in the CA who argued that there was a constructive trust in favour
of the son which bound the bank. Although Denning MR's argument failed, there
are echoes of it in *Lloyds Bank* v. *Carrick* (1996). See above under registered land
for the proposal in Law Commission Paper 254 which envisages that the courts
will still have power to set aside a disposition procured by fraud, and look at the
much criticised registered land case of *Peffer* v. *Rigg* (1978).

■ Rights which are not registrable as land charges

EXAM TIP

You must be *absolutely* clear for the exam if a right is registrable as land charge.

If it is, then check the rules above on the consequences of non-registration.

If not, then we ask if it is:

■ A legal interest? If so, it is binding on a purchaser automatically.

■ An equitable interest? If so, whether it is binding depends on whether the
purchaser was a bona fide purchaser for value without notice.

REVISION NOTE

Check your knowledge of legal and equitable interests in Chapter 1.

Equitable interests

What does bona fide purchaser for value without notice mean?

Bona fide means that the purchaser must be in good faith. It may mean that a person
who buys for an improper purpose would not be protected, but see *Midland Bank* v.
Green (above).

Purchaser for value means that some value must be given and this includes money,
money's worth and marriage. A donee (who takes by gift) would not take free of an
equitable interest.

Notice. This is the most important requirement. Notice means any of the follo

- Actual notice, i.e. actual knowledge.
- Constructive notice. This has two elements:
  (i) A purchaser is bound by any matters which would be revealed by an examination of the deeds. As a result of this rule, it is common for a note of equitable interests to be made on the back of deeds.
  (ii) A purchaser is bound by all matters which would be revealed by an inspection of the land (rule in *Hunt* v. *Luck* (1901).
- Imputed notice. This means that a purchaser has notice of any matters of which his agent has notice as in *Kingsnorth Finance Co. Ltd* v. *Tizard* [1986], where the mortgagee was bound by the knowledge of the surveyor.

> **! Don't be tempted to...**
>
> Don't assume that you need to come to a definite conclusion on whether a purchaser had notice (especially constructive notice) or not. What is vital is to state the rules clearly and apply them to the facts as far as you can.

> **! Don't be tempted to...**
>
> Don't forget that overriding interests *only* arise where title to the land is registered.

■ Summary table

Go through the table below and make sure that you can remember where each right fits in. I am afraid that this is just hard slog!

	Registrable as a land charge?
...its and pr...	No: they are legal interests and bind a purchaser automatically
Interests of a beneficiary under a trust	No: they are equitable interests and so whether they bind a bona fide purchaser depends on notice
Equitable easements and profits (post-1926)	Yes
Equitable easements and profits (pre-1926)	No: they are equitable interests and so whether they bind a bona fide purchaser depends on notice
Restrictive covenants (post-1926)	Yes
Restrictive covenants (pre-1926)	No: they are equitable interests and so whether they bind a bona fide purchaser depends on notice
Estate contracts	Yes
Puisne mortgages	Yes. N.B. these are the only legal interests in this table to require protection as land charges

! Don't be tempted to...

Students often fail to go through problem questions in this area logically. Make sure that you first go to this table and then follow through the consequences of the right being legal or equitable and if it is registrable as a land charge or not. Make sure that you do this.

■Chapter summary: putting it all together

Test yourself

☐ Can you tick all the points from the **revision checklist** at the beginning of this chapter?

☐ Attempt the **sample question** from the beginning of this chapter using the answer guidelines below.

☐ Go to the **companion website** to access more revision support online, including interactive quizzes, sample questions with answer guidelines, 'You be the marker' exercises, flashcards and podcasts you can download.

Answer guidelines

See the problem question at the start of the chapter. A diagram illustrating how to structure your answer is available on the companion website.

Approaching the question

This is the very type of question where a calm logical approach in the exam will pay great dividends!

Assuming that title is registered

■ You must first *identify* the interest: is it legal or equitable? (This also helps when you come to unregistered title.)

■ Then *decide* where it fits in the registration of title to land scheme.

■ Then adopt the same approach for unregistered land.

Important points to include

Assuming that title is registered

Fred : equitable profit – minor interest – needs to be protected by a notice on the register. If not, not binding.

Susie : equitable lease: same as for Fred but if she had actually started to use the land she could claim that she had an overriding interest as a person in occupation under her equitable lease.

Jean – no right to register – just a personal right.

Elsie – may have an overriding interest as a person in actual occupation.

Assuming that title is unregistered

Do the interests need to be registered as land charges?

Fred's profit – yes.

Susie's equitable lease – yes – as an estate contract.

Jean's licence – no – not a proprietary right.

Elsie's right under a trust – no – as it is equitable. However, Elsie's right, unlike Jean's, is a proprietary right. As it is equitable, whether or not John is bound depends on whether he has notice – apply *Kingsnorth Finance Co. Ltd* v. *Tizard*.

 Make your answer stand out

Good knowledge of the relevant case law, especially in relation to Elsie. Spotting that even if Elsie does have an overriding interest John may not be bound by it – apply Sch. 3, para. 2, LRA 2002. You can also make mention of *Bank of Baroda* v. *Dhillon* re Elsie (see Chapter 3).

READ TO IMPRESS

Cooke, *The New Law of Land Registration*, Hart Publishing, Oxford (2003). Chapters 8 (the impact of electronic conveyancing) and 9 (a comparative account of systems of title registration in Europe) are especially recommended.

Dixon, 'Priorities under the Land Registration Act 2002' (2009) 125 LQR 401.

Fergusson, 'Estate contracts, constructive trusts and the Land Charges Act' (1996) 112 LQR 549.

Law Commission paper 254, 'Land registration for the 21st Century – A Consultative Document' (1998).

Law Commission Paper 271, 'Land registration for the 21st Century – a conveyancing revolution' (2001).

Smith, 'The role of registration in modern land law', in Tee (ed.), *Land Law, Issues, Debates, Policy*, Willan, Uffculme (2002).

Thompson, 'The widow's plight' [1996] Conv 295.

NOTES

NOTES

Co-ownership of land

3

■ Topic map

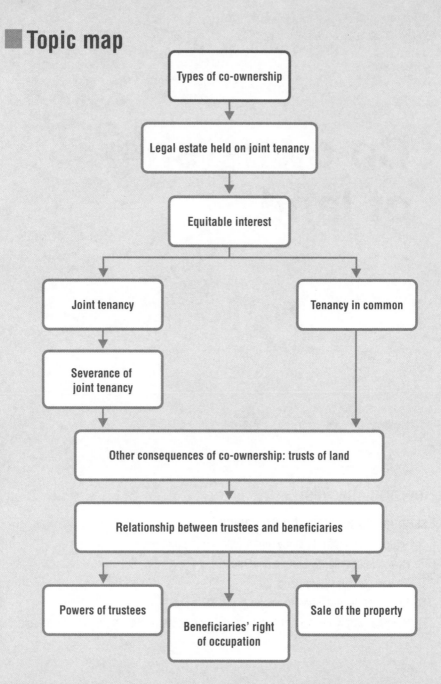

A printable version of this topic map is available from **www.pearsoned.co.uk/lawexpress**

■ Introduction

This area lends itself to problem questions and the issues are relatively straightforward. There are no really major recent cases on the joint tenancy/tenancy in common point but plenty of them on applications for a sale of property.

ASSESSMENT ADVICE

Essay questions A likely topic for an essay is a discussion of the law on trusts of land looking at the position of the trustees and the beneficiaries. You should be able to discuss the case law on powers of the court to order a sale and the link in *Bank of Baroda* v. *Dhillon* with overriding interests. You will find the article by Hopkins (2009) especially useful here.

Problem questions These will probably require the ability to steer a clear path through attempts at severing a joint tenancy. There are a limited number of variations of the theme of how severance can take place and you must know them and be able to apply them.

A problem question may then go on to two other areas: the right of beneficiaries to occupy (check the original purpose for which the property was bought), and applications for a sale.

■ Sample question

Could you answer this question? Below is a typical problem question which could arise on this topic. Guidelines on answering the question are included at the end of the chapter, while a sample essay question and guidance on tackling it can be found on the companion website.

PROBLEM QUESTION

In 2005 John, Mark, Conchetta and Louise were students at Melchester University and had won a prize in the lottery. They used their winnings to buy a house for them all to live in while they completed their studies. The purchase price was £100,000. John contributed £40,000 and the others each paid £20,000. They agreed that the house should belong to them equally and it was registered in the names of them all with a declaration that the survivor could give a receipt for capital money.

Later that year John, having failed to submit an assignment on time, had to leave his course and so he sold his interest in the house to Alf, a fellow student.

Mark got married at Christmas and made a will leaving all his property to his wife Florrie. They went on honeymoon to the seaside but Mark was drowned by a freak wave.

Louise told Conchetta that she could not stand living in the house just with her any more and that she wanted to sell her share. Conchetta was upset by this and a violent quarrel ensued. Louise then went to her solicitor and, acting on his advice, she sent a notice of severance by registered post to Conchetta. When the notice arrived Conchetta was out and so Louise signed for it.

John and Louise now wish to sell the house but Conchetta and Alf wish to a stay.

(a) Advise the parties on the devolution of the legal and equitable interests in the property.
(b) Advise Conchetta and Alf on whether they can remain in the house.
(c) Advise John and Louise on whether they can insist on a sale.

■ Types of co-ownership

This area deals with co-ownership of land. There are three legal concepts which you need to master:

- joint tenancy;
- tenancy in common;
- trusts of land.

All of these can be involved in a problem question.

■ Legal estate held on joint tenancy

Where there is more than one owner of the legal estate, the legal estate must be:

- held by the legal owners as joint tenants;
- held by them on a trust of land.

Four unities are necessary for a joint tenancy to exist:

- time: the interests of all must vest at the same time;
- title: all must derive their title from the same document;

- interest: all must have the same interest;
- possession: all must be equally entitled to possession of the whole land.

KEY DEFINITION: Joint tenancy

Exists where there are no shares, i.e. all the joint tenants own all the land jointly and the four unities are present.

Two vital points:

1 Co-owners cannot hold the legal estate as tenants in common.
2 The distinguishing feature of joint tenancy is the right of survivorship: as joint tenants own no individual share, they cannot leave any part of their joint tenancy by will, nor does it pass under the intestacy rules. Instead it passes to the surviving joint tenants. Section 184 of the LPA 1925 provides that where deaths occur in circumstances making it uncertain which died first then the younger shall be deemed to have survived the elder (see *Hickman* v. *Peacey* (1945) – deaths in a bomb blast).

Example

The legal estate to Blackacre is held by X and Y. This means that:

- They are joint tenants.
- There is a trust of land.

X dies. The legal estate automatically vests in Y only.

Number of joint tenants

KEY STATUTE

Section 34(2), LPA 1925

Where land is conveyed to co-owners who are of full age they:

- must be joint tenants;
- cannot be more than four.

■ Equitable interest

Here there is a choice: it can be held on either:

■ joint tenancy;

■ tenancy in common.

Joint tenancy

This means that the right of survivorship applies to the beneficial interest.

Tenancy in common

KEY DEFINITION: Tenancy in common

Exists where the beneficial owners have shares in the land.

This is the opposite of a joint tenancy. The only unity required is possession. Each is entitled to a separate undivided share and can dispose of this share either during life or on death. Sometimes the four unities are present but there are words of severance and, therefore, there is a tenancy in common.

Remember that in a tenancy in common:

■ there are separate shares;

■ the right of survivorship does not apply.

Example

X and Y hold the legal estate to Blackacre on trust for themselves and Z.

■ The legal title must be held on a joint tenancy.

■ The equitable interest can be held on either a joint tenancy or a tenancy in common.

> If the equitable interest is held on a tenancy in common, X, Y and Z each have a separate share, which they can sell or which can devolve on their death.

How do we tell if there is a joint tenancy or a tenancy in common?

The question may make it clear.

Example

X and Y agree that if they die their interest in the property shall go to the other.

This agreement overrides anything else such as unequal contributions to the purchase price and there will be a joint tenancy as the parties intend that the right of survivorship shall apply.

The question may not make it clear and so you must look for:

Words of severance

Even if the four unities exist there will not be a joint tenancy if there are words of severance, i.e. words which indicate that the parties are to hold separate shares. Examples are:

- 'in equal shares': *Payne* v. *Webb* (1874);
- 'equally': *Lewen* v. *Dodd* (1595);
- 'to be divided between': *Peat* v. *Chapman* (1750).

Presumptions of equity

If there are no words of severance, then look at this:

Equity leans against a joint tenancy and the law leans against a tenancy in common.

In the following cases equity presumes that there is a tenancy in common:

- purchase in unequal shares: *Lake* v. *Gibson* (1729); *Bull* v. *Bull* (1955);
- where there is a relationship of a commercial character, e.g. partnership property: *Re Fuller* (1933);
- where money is lent on mortgage by two or more persons, they are presumed to hold the estate which they receive by way of security as tenants in common: *Morley* v. *Bird* (1798).

Remember: if there is an express agreement that the parties will hold as joint tenants, this will override any of the above presumptions.

EXAM TIP

Always refer to a joint tenant as having an interest but a tenant in common as having a share.

▇ Severance of joint tenancy

Severance of an equitable joint tenancy to turn it into a tenancy in common

EXAM TIP

Problem questions frequently require you to look at this area. As a useful guide, the situation in the question usually involves a joint tenancy as it can be severed.

KEY STATUTE

Section 3(4), Administration of Estates Act 1925

Severance cannot be effected by will.

There are two ways to sever a joint tenancy:

- by notice in writing;
- in equity.

By notice in writing

KEY STATUTE

Section 36(2), LPA 1925

A joint tenant may give notice of intention to sever to all other joint tenants.

Any notice must be in writing (s. 196(1), LPA 1925) and giving notice means serving notice (s. 196(3) and (4), LPA 1925).

See *Re 88 Berkeley Road* (1971) and *Kinch* v. *Bullard* (1999).

In equity

KEY DEFINITION: Severance in equity

'Such acts or things as would, in the case of personal estate, sever the tenancy in equity' (*Williams* v. *Hensman* (1861)).

In *Williams* v. *Hensman* (1861) Page-Wood VC said that there are three methods:

1 An act of any one of the parties operating on his own share, e.g. a sale of the joint tenant's beneficial interest or the bankruptcy of a joint tenant. In equity a sale will take place as soon as there is a specifically enforceable contract to sell.

Example

X sells his beneficial interest in Blackacre to W. This severs X's interest in equity and so W is a tenant in common.

! Don't be tempted to...

Students often think that when an equitable joint tenant sells his interest he also ceases to be a holder of the legal estate. This is wrong – it is unaffected. So in the above example, X will only cease to hold the legal estate if there is a transfer to the other joint tenants.

2 Mutual agreement. In *Burgess* v. *Rawnsley* (1975) an oral agreement by one joint tenant to purchase the share of the other operated to sever even though the contract was not specifically enforceable as there was nothing in writing. See also *Hunter* v. *Burbage* (1994).
3 Any other course of dealing which shows that the interests of all were mutually treated as constituting a tenancy in common. In *Burgess* Sir John Pennycuick said that it includes negotiations which, although not resulting in an agreement, indicate a common intention to sever. Denning MR said that it included a course of dealing in which one party makes it clear to the others that he 'desires that their shares should no longer be held jointly but be held in common', but Pennycuick's view seems to represent the law.

> **!** **Don't be tempted to...**
>
> Students often overlook that any agreement or common intention must be between *all* of the co-owners. This is a common examination point. Check the question carefully to see if this is so.

Forfeiture

If one joint tenant kills another, the right of survivorship should not operate, as this would allow the murderer to benefit from his act.

■ Other consequences of co-ownership: trust of land

Trusts of land

Once the question of who holds the legal title has been dealt with, one can then turn to the question of the terms on which it is held. The answer is that under the Trusts of Land and Appointment of Trustees Act 1996 (TLATA), a trust of land automatically comes into existence whenever the legal title to land is held by joint tenants (s. 36(1), LPA, as amended by the TLATA).

Note that until TLATA came into force land held on trust was held on a trust for sale.

The following are the main provisions of the TLATA and all references to sections are to sections of that Act.

> **EXAM TIP**
>
> In an exam, you will need to be able to apply these statutory provisions. It is essential is that you know what area each section deals with and how they relate to each other.

Relationship between trustees and beneficiaries

Powers of trustees

Trustees have all the powers of an absolute owner of land (s. 6(1) TLATA) but, as trustees, they are bound by the fiduciary duties of trustees when exercising their functions. As Megarry VC put it in *Cowan* v. *Scargill* (1984): 'they must put the interests of the beneficiaries first.'

Section 6, TLATA 1996

Confers two specific powers on trustees:
- **(a)** to purchase land by way of investment for the occupation of any beneficiary or for any other reason;
- **(b)** to transfer the land to the beneficiaries when they are all of full age and capacity even though they have not requested this.

Exclusion and restriction of powers

Section 8(1), TLATA 1996

This allows the settlor to exclude all or any of the provisions of s. 6.

Delegation by trustees

Section 9, TLATA 1996

This provides that the trustees may, by power of attorney, delegate any of their functions relating to land to a beneficiary of full age and capacity who is entitled to an interest in possession in land. Any delegation must be unanimous and, therefore, only one trustee can revoke it as this destroys unanimity. If trustees refuse to delegate, an application may be made to the court under s. 14 by a beneficiary for an order that a delegation should be made. Any delegate beneficiary has the same duties as an actual trustee.

Consultation with beneficiaries

Section 11(1), TLATA 1996

This provides that trustees must 'so far as practicable' consult the beneficiaries of full age who are beneficially entitled to an interest in possession in the land and 'so far as is consistent with the general interest of the trust' to give effect to those wishes or, in cases of dispute, the wishes of the majority, according to the value of their combined interests.

Beneficiaries' rights of occupation

KEY STATUTE

Section 12, TLATA 1996

This gives a right of occupation to beneficiaries who are entitled to an interest in possession in the land, provided that the trust so allows but no right of occupation arises if the land is either unavailable or unsuitable for occupation by the beneficiary in question.

KEY STATUTE

Section 13, TLATA 1996

This allows the trustees power to exclude or restrict the right to occupy but the power must not be exercised unreasonably. Conditions may be imposed on occupation and s. 13(5) sets out examples: paying outgoings and complying with obligations, e.g. ensuring that any planning permission is complied with. Section 13(4) sets out matters to which the trustees must have regard when exercising their powers to restrict or exclude the right to occupy: intentions of the settlor, purposes for which the land is held on trust and the circumstances and wishes of beneficiaries who would be entitled to occupy but for the exclusion or restriction. Section 13(7) provides that a person in occupation of the land, whether or not in occupation under s. 12, shall not be evicted except with their consent or a court order. This includes those in occupation under other rights than those of a trust beneficiary, e.g. a matrimonial home right under the Family Law Act 1996. The court, when deciding whether to evict, may, by s. 13(8) have regard to the matters set out in s. 13(4).

■ Sale of the property
Powers of the court to order a sale

These are contained in the following sections: s. 14 deals with who can apply and s. 15 with the principles on which the court can order a sale.

KEY STATUTE

Section 14, TLATA 1996

This allows any person interested in the trust to apply to the court for an order, which could, e.g., be for a sale (see below), or authorising what would otherwise be a breach of trust. The term 'any person interested' includes trustees, beneficiaries, remaindermen and secured creditors of beneficiaries.

KEY STATUTE

Section 15(1), TLATA 1996

This sets out the following criteria to which the courts must have regard when settling disputes (in practice, and certainly in examination questions, these are particularly relevant when looking at disputes over whether land should be sold):

(a) the intentions of the settlor;
(b) the purposes for which the property is held on trust;
(c) the welfare of any minor who either occupies, or might reasonably be expected to occupy, the land as his home;
(d) the interests of any secured creditor of any beneficiary.

KEY CASE

Bank of Ireland Home Mortgages Ltd v. *Bell* [2001] 2 All ER (Comm) 920 (CA)
Concerning: application of the principles in s. 15, TLATA

Facts

The family home was owned jointly by the husband (H) and wife (W) in law but the wife had only a 10% beneficial interest. H forged W's signature on a mortgage and then left W. She remained in the house with their son for 10 years after H stopped making mortgage repayments, and when the bank sought possession, W was in poor health.

Legal principle

The mortgage debt was now £300,000 and a sale would be ordered, as a 'powerful consideration' was 'whether the creditor is receiving proper recompense for being kept out of his money'. This was clearly not the case.

Compare this case with the earlier one of *Mortgage Corporation* v. *Shaire* (2001), where Neuberger J. said that 'By comparison with the previous law' (i.e. in the LPA 1925), Parliament had intended to 'tip the scales more in favour of families and against banks and other chargees'.

KEY CASE

Bank of Baroda v. *Dhillon* [1998] 1 FLR 524 (HC)

Concerning: relationship between s. 15, TLATA and overriding interests

Facts

A bank applied for an order for sale of the matrimonial home.

Legal principle

This would be granted even though the wife had an overriding interest under the LRA 1925 (now Sch. 3, para. 2, LRA 2002) which bound the bank. The crucial factor was that the children were grown up and after the sale W would still have enough money for other accommodation.

REVISION NOTE

Check your knowledge of overriding interests in Chapter 2 and note the reference to *Bank of Baroda* v. *Dhillon.*

An early case on s. 30, LPA, but which is probably still good law, is *Re Buchanan – Wollaston's Conveyance* (1939), where land was bought by four co-owners to prevent it from being built on. One later wished to sell but the others did not. As the original purpose remained the court refused to order a sale.

Read *Barca* v. *Mears* (2004) on the relationship between ss. 14 and 15, TLATA, and the Human Rights Act (Article 8 – respect for private and family life).

■ **Chapter summary**: putting it all together

Test yourself

- ☐ Can you tick all the points from the **revision checklist** at the beginning of this chapter?
- ☐ Attempt the **sample question** from the beginning of this chapter using the answer guidelines below.
- ☐ Go to the **companion website** to access more revision support online, including interactive quizzes, sample questions with answer guidelines, 'you be the marker' exercises, flashcards and podcasts you can download.

Answer guidelines

See problem question at the start of the chapter. A diagram illustrating how to structure your answer is available on the companion website.

Approaching the question

- ■ Part (a): apply the rules on joint tenancies and tenancies in common – all that is required is a clear understanding of the law and a logical approach.
- ■ Parts (b) and (c): here, especially in (c), there is scope for discussion of case law and so more chance to earn vital extra marks!

Important points to include

Stage one: John sells his interest in the house to Alf, a fellow student.

Stage two: Mark gets married and makes a will leaving all his property to Florrie, and is then drowned.

Stage three: Louise tells Conchita that she cannot stand living in the house, etc. There is no severance. Rights remain the same.

Stage four: Louise serves notice of severance.

- Part (a): Follow through the situation as above. Note that inequality of contributions does not make them tenants in common in equity, as their agreement plus the declaration at the Land Registry override this. Apply *Burgess* v. *Rawnsley* to the need for an agreement between Louise and Conchetta and *Re 88 Berkeley Road* to the receipt of the notice by Louise.
- Part (b): Right to occupy: apply s. 12, TLATA (also s. 11 – need for consultation). If Alf has no right to occupy, then s. 13 – right can be restricted.
- Part (c): Cannot insist on sale. Apply s. 14 (right to apply) and s. 15 (principles on which a sale can be ordered).

✓ Make your answer stand out

- Mention the possible application of the Human Rights Act.
- Link with overriding interests.
- Discuss in depth the case law on s. 15, TLATA.

READ TO IMPRESS

Dixon, 'Trusts of land, bankruptcy and human rights' [2005] Conv 161.

Fox, 'Creditors and the concept of the family home: a functional analysis' (2005) 25 LS 201.

Hopkins, 'Regulating trusts of the home: private law and social policy' (2009) 125 LQR 310.

Tee, 'Severance revisited' [1995] Conv 104.

NOTES

NOTES

Trusts and the home

4

■Topic map

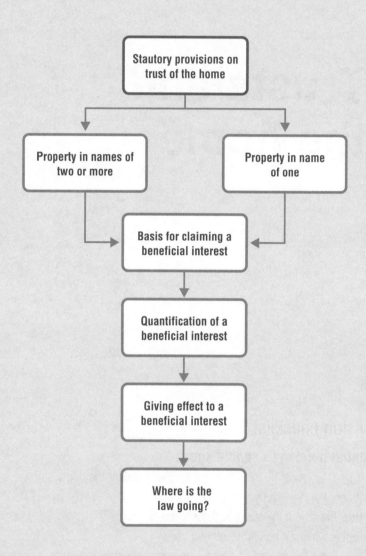

A printable version of this topic map is available from **www.pearsoned.co.uk/lawexpress**

■Introduction

This chapter deals with the part played by equity in disputes over the home. It is most likely to feature as a problem question in a land law examination where it may well be linked with a point about land registration. It could also be an essay question. It is also an excellent topic to consider at this stage as it also involves you in revising material covered in Chapters 1, 2 and 3.

ASSESSMENT ADVICE

Essay questions This can be a topic in examination questions but much will depend on the extent to which this topic is taught in the equity course. However, a land law exam may ask you to discuss the present state of the law in the light of earlier approaches.

Problem questions In problem questions you need to separate two issues:

■ Acquisition – what, if any, beneficial interest in the property has a party acquired?

■ Quantification – assuming that a beneficial interest has been acquired, how is it quantified?

Then look first at the facts and see if the parties are seeking a divorce or an order on the breakdown of a civil partnership (under the Civil Partnerships Act 2004 the court has the same powers to make orders on the breakdown of a registered civil partnership as it does on a divorce). If so, then the law of property is not relevant and the matter comes under family law. Otherwise, it is.

A problem question in the exam typically involves cohabitees but can involve married partners where the issue is not distribution of assets on a divorce but rather, for example, the house was mortgaged and the issue is the rights of one party to the marriage against the lender. Another possibility is where parents have contributed to the purchase of a house which is in the name of their children.

Once you have decided that a party does have a beneficial interest, you must go on to look at the rules for deciding their share.

In addition – and this is where a problem question in land law is likely to differ from one on this area in an equity exam – the question may also ask you to decide

> if, assuming that a party does have a beneficial interest in the land, that interest is binding on a purchaser. Here you will need to consider whether title to the land is registered or not and refer to Chapter 2. You may also need to use the detail in Chapter 3 on the rights contained in the TLATA of beneficiaries and others in land held on trust.

■ Sample question

Could you answer this question? Below is a typical problem question that could arise on this topic. Guidelines on answering the question are included at the end of this chapter, while a sample essay question and guidance on tackling it can be found on the companion website.

PROBLEM QUESTION

Robert and Josephine met in 2006 and decided to set up home together. They bought 'The Laurels', a registered freehold property, for £300,000 with the aid of a mortgage of £100,000 from the Friendly Building Society secured by a legal charge over the property. Josephine was registered as sole proprietor as Robert's earnings as a proofreader fluctuated greatly. Robert contributed 5% of the deposit from his savings but Josephine paid the rest and she initially assumed responsibility for the mortgage repayments.

In 2007 Robert said to Josephine: 'I realise what a financial drain these payments must be to you. From now on, I will pay all the utility bills so that your earnings are used for the mortgage repayments'. Josephine replied: 'It's about time that you contributed to our joint venture'. Robert, feeling guilty after Josephine's words, then started to begin work on an extension to the house to give them extra room when their family arrived.

In 2008 Josephine needed money to expand a business venture of hers and so, while Robert was on a six-month expedition to Tibet, she took out a loan from the Newtown Bank secured by a second legal charge on 'The Laurels'.

Advise Robert what rights, if any, he has in respect of 'The Laurels'.

Would it make any difference to your answer if title to 'The Laurels' was unregistered?

Note: You should be aware that this problem question is probably *longer* than you might find in the exam as a last section has been included asking you of the position if title to the house was unregistered. This is to make sure that you recall the difference between registered and unregistered land!

The law of trusts and the home

An exam question often revolves around the following scenario, which involves both this chapter and Chapter 2.

There are two issues:

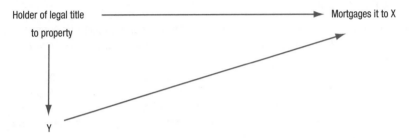

Holder of legal title to property   →   Mortgages it to X

Y

Claims to have a beneficial interest in the property

- Does Y have a beneficial interest? This is dealt with in this chapter.
- If Y does have a beneficial interest, then whether X is bound by it will depend on the rules for registered land (Chapter 2 – especially the law on overriding interests) or unregistered land (Chapter 2 – especially the doctrine of notice – see, for example *Kingsnorth Finance Co. Ltd* v. *Tizard* (1986)).

> **EXAM TIP**
>
> Note that in *Stack* v. *Dowden* (discussed in detail below) the HL dealt with a situation where the house was in the names of both parties to a relationship and the issue was the extent of their respective shares. Watch for this variation in an exam.

First, you need to be aware of the following statutory provisions:

> **EXAM TIP**
>
> In any problem question you need to point out, near the start of your answer, the relevance of the statutory provisions on the creation of trusts of land.

KEY STATUTE

> ### Section 53(1)(b), LPA 1925
>
> Declaration of a trust of land must be in writing or there must be written evidence of it.
>
> ### Section 53(2), LPA 1925
>
> The requirement in s. 53(1)(b) does not apply to resulting, implied or constructive trusts. This is why trusts of the kind discussed below are not affected by the need for writing.

If there is an express declaration of trust which satisfies s. 53(1)(b), then this is conclusive unless varied by subsequent agreement or affected by proprietary estoppel (*Goodman* v. *Gallant* (1986)).

Here are two examples of possible claims. Keep them in mind as you go through the law.

> ## Example one
>
> John and his partner, Joan, live at Pine Lodge. The house is in John's name but Joan contributed 10% of the deposit when John bought it and her earnings as a solicitor pay the household bills enabling John's income as a plumber to be used to pay off the mortgage. They have no children.
>
> Joan claims a share in the property.

> ## Example two
>
> Fred and his partner, Molly, live at Stone Cottage. The house was bought by Molly in 1990 and Fred moved in with her in 1993. They have five children. Molly is an interior designer and she and Fred decided that in view of her greater earning power she should continue to work and Fred would stay at home and look after their five children. Thus Molly's earnings both pay off the mortgage and all other bills.
>
> Fred claims a share in the property.

At the outset of the answer to a problem question, clear the ground and check whether it is:

Situation one: the property is held in the names of two or more persons and the claim concerns the extent of their beneficial shares. If so, the exact ratio of *Stack* v. *Dowden* will apply.

Situation two: the property is held in the names of one person and the claim is by another person who claims a beneficial interest. If so, the principles stated in *Stack* v. *Dowden,* particularly by Lady Hale, will apply.

You will see that in both examples one and two above situation two applies.

Summary of points to consider

(a) On what basis can a beneficial interest be claimed?
(b) The debate on how the courts decide whether the parties had any common intention regarding the beneficial interests in the property.
(c) The distinction, which is not always made clear by the courts, between the rules for deciding acquisition and quantification of the beneficial interests.

On what basis can a beneficial interest be claimed?

There are three possibilities:

(a) **Resulting trust.** This approach will be most appropriate where the claim is based on contributions to the cost of acquisition of the property and the effect will be that the beneficial shares of the parties will be in proportion to their respective contributions.
(b) **Constructive trust.** This approach will be most appropriate where the claim is based on factors other than, or in addition to, contributions to the cost of acquisition of the property and the courts, when deciding quantification, can take account of factors other than the cost of acquisition.
(c) **Estoppel.** This does not usually arise as a separate issue and is often linked to the imposition of a constructive trust in, for example, *Lloyds Bank* v. *Rosset* (1991). Note a case where estoppel was pleaded and failed: *H* v. *M* (2004).

> **REVISION NOTE**
>
> Check Chapter 5 to revise your knowledge of estoppel.

In example one above under the resulting trust approach Joan would receive a beneficial interest but it would only take account of her contributions to the cost of acquisition. In example two Fred would receive nothing under the resulting trust approach. Both Joan and Fred would be better off under the constructive trust.

The fundamental question for the courts to decide is: what was the common intention of the parties and not what would be fair as between them. Keep stressing this in the exam.

Situation one: where the property is held in the names of two or more persons and the claim concerns the extent of their beneficial shares

---

KEY CASE

Stack v. *Dowden* [2007] UKHL 17 (HL)

Concerning: principles to be applied when deciding the extent of beneficial interests in property where the legal title is held in joint names

Facts

The legal title to the house was in joint names (i.e. held as joint tenants). X (the woman) had contributed 65% of the price and the other 35% was provided by a joint loan secured on the legal title held by her and Y (the man). There was no restriction entered on the register and the assumption was that they were equitable joint tenants.

Legal principles

Lady Hale held that a conveyance in joint names established a *prima facie* case of a 50:50 split and the burden is on the person seeking to show that the parties did intend their beneficial interests to be different from their legal interests to prove this. This case was unusual in that X had contributed far more to the purchase than Y and they had kept their financial affairs rigidly separate and so a 65:35 split was justified. The fundamental principle, in Lady Hale's words, is 'to ascertain the parties' shared intentions, actual, inferred or imputed, with respect to the property in the light of their whole course of conduct in relation to it'.

She laid down a number of factors, which she pointed out are not exhaustive, to be considered in deciding this question:

- (a) any advice or discussions at the time of the transfer which cast light upon their intentions;
- (b) the reasons why the home was acquired in their joint names;
- (c) the reasons why (if it be the case) the survivor was authorised to give a receipt for the capital moneys;
- (d) the purpose for which the home was acquired;
- (e) the nature of the parties' relationship;
- (f) whether they had children for whom they both had responsibility to provide a home;

(g) how the purchase was financed, both initially and subsequently;
(h) how the parties arranged their finances, whether separately or together or a bit of both;
(i) how they discharged the outgoings on the property and their other household expenses.

! Don't be tempted to...

Make sure you understand the debate about exactly how the 'common intention' of the parties is to be ascertained. Note Lady Hale's words above: 'the parties' shared intentions, actual, inferred or imputed.' Does the word 'imputed' allow the courts to decide what the parties' intentions were? Finding a common intention is often artificial as the reality is that people do not usually discuss these matters when property is acquired as they do not anticipate their relationship coming to an end. See two articles: Clarke (1992) and Gardner (1993).

 Make your answer stand out

Read the speech of Lord Neuberger, who dissented and who held that the correct approach was a resulting trust. He was also one of the judges in *Laskar* v. *Laskar* (below).

Stack v. *Dowden* was applied in *Fowler* v. *Barron* (2008), where on the facts the presumption of a 50:50 split in the beneficial ownership was not rebutted.

Make your answer stand out

Look carefully at the facts of this case. Was a different result from that in *Stack* justified?

KEY CASE

Laskar v. *Laskar* [2008] EWCA Civ 347

Concerning: application of Stack v. *Dowden where property was purchased as an investment*

Facts

Property was bought as an investment by A but she could not raise the funds necessary to purchase the property and, in order to secure a mortgage, she transferred the property into the names of herself and her daughter B.

Legal principle

As the property was bought as an investment the presumption that each joint tenant was entitled to an equal proportion of the beneficial interest would not apply and instead a resulting trust was imposed and each party was entitled to the value of her own contribution.

Situation two: where the property is held in the names of one person and the claim is by another person who claims a beneficial interest

KEY CASE

Stack v. Dowden [2007] UKHL 17

Concerning: principles to be applied when deciding the extent of beneficial interests in property where the legal title is held in the name of one party and other parties claim a beneficial interest

Facts

These were given above.

Legal principle

The same factors will apply as in situation one with the exception of those which are clearly only relevant to situation one: (b) and (c) are suggested.

An example of the approach in *Stack* v. *Dowden* to a situation two case is *Abbott* v. *Abbott* (2007).

In *Stack* v. *Dowden* Lord Walker said that 'the law has moved on, and your Lordships should move it a little more in the same direction' from the decision in *Lloyds Bank* v. *Rosset* (1991). However, this case involved the same fundamental principle as in

Stack v. *Dowden* – i.e. how to ascertain the common intentions of the parties – and is still often referred to. You should certainly mention it in an essay question on the development of the law, and the principles in it may also be useful in a problem question although *Stack* v. *Dowden* is now the main authority.

Look at recent cases in this area: in *Jones* v. *Kernott* (2009) the *Stack* v. *Dowden* approach was applied; in *James* v. *Thomas* (2007) the claim failed and it is arguable that it would have done so on either *Stack* v. *Dowden* or *Lloyds Bank* v. *Rosset* principles.

In examples one and two above both Joan and Fred would be able to refer to the list set out by Lady Hale in *Stack* v. *Dowden* in support of their claims. Consider whether they would both be likely to be better or worse off under the principles in *Lloyds Bank* v. *Rosset*.

 Make your answer stand out

An essay on the development of the law in this area is a possibility. Look at previous attempts to provide a satisfactory solution such as *Eves* v. *Eves* (1975). A case which is often said to illustrate the unfairness of this area of the law is *Burns* v. *Burns* (1984).

■ Quantification of the beneficial interest

EXAM TIP

Make sure that you deal with this completely separately from the preceding question of whether a party has a beneficial interest at all. Do not confuse the two!

The leading authority is *Oxley* v. *Hiscock* (2004), where Chadwick LJ said that: 'each is entitled to that share which the court considers fair having regard to the whole course of dealing between them in relation to the property.' And in that context, 'the whole course of dealing between them in relation to the property' includes the arrangements which they make from time to time in order to meet the outgoings (for example, mortgage contributions, council tax and utilities, repairs, insurance and housekeeping) which have to be met if they are to live in the property as their home.

Note that the use by Chadwick LJ of the word 'fair' shows that this approach is a broad one and is based, to some extent, on judicial discretion. Also, although the decision predates *Stack* v. *Dowden*, it was approved in that case and in *Fowler* v. *Barron*.

■ Giving effect to the beneficial interest of a party

In a problem question you should point out that as this is equity the beneficial interest will be held on a tenancy in common unless there is an intention to hold joint tenants as seemed to be the case in *Stack* v. *Dowden*. See *Bull* v. *Bull* (1955).

■ Where is the law in England and Wales going?

The Law Commission in its report No. 307, 'Cohabitation: the Financial Consequences of Relationship Breakdown' proposed a scheme where parties to a relationship could claim on the basis of:

- **economic advantage** (the retention of some economic benefit arising from contributions made by the other party during the relationship); or

- **economic disadvantage** (economic sacrifices made as result of that party's contribution to the relationship or resulting from continuing child-care responsibilities following separation).

The effect would have been to widen the net for possible claimants. Look at *Burns* v. *Burns* and see if the claimant would have succeeded under these proposals. However, on 6 March 2008 the Government announced that it was delaying any implementation of the scheme until it had assessed research findings on the effect of the Family Law (Scotland) Act 2006 which has similar provisions. In fact the changes in the law made by *Stack* v. *Dowden* may make the need for legislation less pressing.

✓ Make your answer stand out

You will boost your marks by knowledge of the position in other jurisdictions. The articles by Gardner (1993) and Rotherham (2004) – see further reading; below – will give you some information. In brief the courts adopt wider approaches than has been the case in England, at least until *Stack* v. *Dowden*. See, for example:

- *Soulos* v. *Korkontzilas* (1997) – Canada: remedial constructive trust and unjust enrichment.

- *Gilles* v. *Keogh* (1989) – New Zealand: meeting the reasonable expectations of the parties but is it now? See Rotherham (2004).

- *Baumgartner* v. *Baumgartner* (1987) and *Muchinski* v. *Dodds* (1981) – Australia: unconscionability.

■Chapter summary: putting it all together

Test yourself

☐ Can you tick all the points from the **revision checklist** at the beginning of this chapter?

☐ Attempt the **sample question** from the beginning of this chapter using the answer guidelines below.

☐ Go to the **companion website** to access more revision support online, including interactive quizzes, sample questions with answer guidelines, 'you be the marker' exercises, flashcards and podcasts you can download.

Answer guidelines

See the problem question at the start of the chapter. A diagram illustrating how to structure your answer is available on the companion website.

Approaching the question

This question involves two areas and you must spend time on each in order to gain a good pass. Do not rush into the issue of whether Robert's beneficial interest binds the mortgagees before you decide if he has a beneficial interest at all.

Does Robert have a beneficial interest? Consider the following:

■ The parties are not married – nor is there any express declaration of trust to satisfy s. 53(1)(b), LPA 1925 – so Robert's claim must be under a resulting/ constructive trust and/or estoppel.

■ This is situation two (above) and the likely claim is under a constructive trust – is there a common intention regarding the beneficial interests? Note that Josephine referred to 'our joint venture' some time after acquisition. Does this make a difference?

Important points to include

- *Stack* v. *Dowden* – apply Lady Hale's reasoning. Likely that Robert will succeed.

Then consider:

- Size of the share – *Oxley* v. *Hiscock*.
- Robert may be a tenant in common in equity of 'The Laurels' and entitled to share in the proceeds of sale.

Then consider whether Robert's rights are binding on:

(a) The first mortgagee – Friendly Building Society. No, he gets no interest in the property until completion – *Abbey National* v. *Cann* and *Paddington BS* v. *Mendelsohn* (see Chapter 2).

(b) The second mortgagee – Newtown Bank. This is a post-acquisition mortgage so Robert's interest may be binding if it overrides that of the bank. Apply Sch. 3, para. 22, LRA 2002 and note that Robert's absence may not deprive him of his interest – *Chhokar* v. *Chhokar* (see Chapter 2).

If Robert's interest does bind the bank, Robert does have a right to occupy under s. 12 of TLATA, but the bank could still apply for a sale – apply s. 14 of the TLATA and the criteria in s. 15 together with *Bank of Baroda* v. *Dhillon* (see Chapter 3).

If title was unregistered then answer (a) above would be the same but, as far as the Newtown Bank is concerned, Robert's equitable interest would be binding on it if it had notice – *Kingsnorth Finance Co.* v. *Tizard* – interests under trusts are not registrable as land charges (see Chapters 1 and 2).

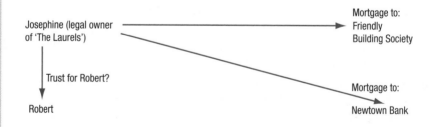

Mortgage to:
Friendly
Building Society

Josephine (legal owner
of 'The Laurels')

Trust for Robert?

Mortgage to:

Robert

Newtown Bank

Make your answer stand out

Mention one or more of the following in your answer:

- Case law post-*Stack* v. *Dowden*.
- *Rosset* principles.
- Lord Neuberger's divergent view in *Stack* v. *Dowden*.
- Law Commission's proposals.

READ TO IMPRESS

Clarke, 'The family home, intention and agreement' (1992) Fam Law 72.

Dixon, 'Resulting and constructive trusts of land; the mist descends and rises' [2005] Conv 79.

Dixon, 'The never-ending story – co-ownership after *Stack* v. *Dowden*' [2007] Conv 456.

Gardner, 'Rethinking family property' (1993) 109 LQR 263.

Law Commission Report 307, 'Cohabitation: the financial consequences of relationship breakdown' (2007).

Rotherham, 'The property rights of unmarried cohabitees: a case for reform' [2004] Conv 268. Excellent general survey.

Swadling, 'The common intention constructive trust in the House of Lords: an opportunity missed' (2007) LQR 511.

NOTES

NOTES

Licences and proprietary estoppel

5

Revision checklist

Essential points you should know:

- [ ] Distinction between licences and property rights
- [ ] Types of licences
- [ ] Do contractual licences create interests in land?
- [ ] When proprietary estoppel can create a licence
- [ ] Conditions for proprietary estoppel to apply

■ Topic map

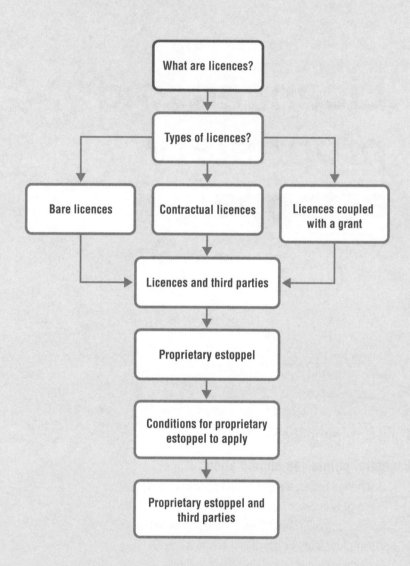

A printable version of this topic map is available from **www.pearsoned.co.uk/lawexpress**

■Introduction

This chapter deals with two areas which may be linked in a question on estoppel licences or which may be the subject of two different questions – one on licences and one on estoppel. The area of estoppel has been the subject of recent significant case law and you must have a thorough knowledge of this for the exam. Licences link to leases (Chapter 6) while estoppel links to trusts of the home (Chapter 4).

ASSESSMENT ADVICE

Essay question will usually ask you about:

■ The status of licences (see also the material on leases in Chapter 6);

■ The extent to which a licence can confer a proprietary right;

■ The nature of estoppel.

Problem questions could be on:

■ *Whether a licence binds a third party.* Here it is essential that you are clear on what the present law *is* and what the law *was*!

■ *An estoppel situation.* Here you need to be absolutely clear on the requirements for estoppel to apply and be able to use the cases well. It may well be linked to the question of whether the estoppel right binds third parties.

■Sample question

Could you answer this question? Below is a typical problem question that could arise on this topic. Guidelines on answering the question are included at the end of this chapter, whilst a sample essay question and guidance on tackling it can be found on the companion website.

PROBLEM QUESTION

Emily is the daughter of Claire, who has recently died. When Claire was aged 50, Emily gave up her job as a solicitor to move in and look after her mother, and she continued to do this until Claire died, aged 82. Claire was disabled and there was an informal arrangement that Claire's incapacity benefit would be paid to Emily to meet the needs of them both. In addition, Emily drew a carer's allowance for looking after her mother. Utility and other bills were paid out of Claire's savings.

Claire often said to Emily: 'I don't know what I would do without you. When I am gone you will have a secure home.' Emily assumed that Claire meant that she would leave her the house.

Claire has died intestate and has left seven children, including Emily, and under the intestacy rules the house will go to them equally.

Advise Emily on whether she has any rights in the house which are binding on the other children.

Would your answer differ if all the other children had signed a document 10 years ago stating that, when Claire died, they would allow Emily to remain at the house?

■ What are licences?

KEY DEFINITION: Licence

This is permission from an owner of land (licensor) to the licensee to use the land for an agreed purpose.

In general, licences are different from all the other rights in this book as they are not property rights. Note this principle from *Thomas* v. *Sorrell* (1673): 'A licence properly passeth no interest nor alters or transfers property in any thing' (Vaughan CJ).

REVISION NOTE

Check that you are familiar with the idea of proprietary rights over the land as distinct from personal rights.

The distinction between leases and licences is explored in Chapter 6.

There are various types of licences:

Bare licences

KEY DEFINITION: Bare licences

Licences given without any consideration from the licensee, i.e. when you are invited to someone's house for a party. They can be withdrawn by the licensor at any time.

Licences coupled with a grant

KEY DEFINITION: Licences coupled with a grant

Where the licence is linked to an interest in the land, e.g. a licence to go on to land to collect wood. The right to collect wood is a profit.

It is misleading to talk at all of licences here as the right to go on to the land is really part of the profit. These licences will last as long as the right to which they are attached.

 Make your answer stand out

In *Hurst* v. *Picture Theatres Ltd* (1915) the court held that a cinema ticket could grant an interest in land but this was criticised by Latham CJ in the Australian case of *Cowell* v. *Rosehill Racecourse* (1937), where he pointed out that the decision in *Hurst* 'ignores the distinction between a personal and a property right'. *Hurst* was really a contractual licence.

Contractual licences

KEY DEFINITION: Contractual licence

Where a licence is given for valuable consideration.

! Don't be tempted to...

Make sure that you are clear on when licences can be revoked. At common law contractual licences and bare licences can in principle be revoked at any time, although equitable remedies may be used to restrain a breach. There is no problem with bare licences, but where a person has paid for a licence, it has seemed unfair for it to be capable of being revoked and this has led to a good deal of case law, beginning with *Wood* v. *Leadbitter* (1845), a case which makes a good starting point for essay questions.

Example

I pay £100 for a ticket to a test match. I am just starting to enjoy the game when an attendant tells me to leave. I am just told to go with no reason and, when I refuse, I am forcibly ejected. It seems that I had been mistaken for someone else who was a troublemaker.

KEY CASE

Winter Gardens Theatre (London) Ltd v. *Millennium Productions Ltd* [1947] 2 All ER331 (HL)

Concerning: the revocability of licences

Facts

The owners of a theatre licensed it for six months to Millennium Productions but later gave them one month's notice to leave, after Millennium Productions had contracted with a production company for it to put on a play at the theatre for six months.

Legal principle

A licence can be revoked on giving reasonable notice and here the revocation was valid.

The topic of revocability of licences is a favourite one in essays and you should read the different cases carefully. Make sure that you stress this one simple point: could a licence be revoked (cancelled) at any time or should it be treated as an interest in land, like other land law rights? If it can be revoked, is notice required?

Licences are also important in connection with leases as a licensee of property has no security of tenure. Check Chapter 6 to make sure that you understand this. You could bring this point in to your essay on licences.

Equitable remedies to prevent revocation of a licence

When equitable remedies became available in all courts after the Judicature Acts 1873–5 equitable remedies became available, in particular, injunctions and specific performance, to protect a licensee. In *Winter Gardens Theatre (London) Ltd* v. *Millennium Productions* the HL said, obiter, that where a contractual licence is, on its terms, irrevocable, then revocation in breach of contract can be restrained by injunction. Note especially *Verrall* v. *Great Yarmouth Borough Council* (1980) as an example of the use of an equitable remedy to enforce a licence.

◼ Licences and third parties

In an answer start by distinguishing between:

- Bare licences – cannot bind third parties.
- Licences coupled with a grant. If the grant confers a proprietary interest in land then the licence, as linked to the grant, will bind third parties.
- Contractual licences – this is the problem area.

Licenses and third parties is a favourite topic for essay questions.

This case lays down the orthodox view:

King v. *David Allen Ltd* [1916] 2 AC 54 (HL)
Concerning: whether a contractual licence is binding on third parties

Facts

A licence was granted allowing the fixing of advertisements to the wall of a cinema. The licensor then granted a lease of the cinema to a third party.

Legal principle

The grant of the lease had ended the contractual licence.

Note attempts by the courts to make contractual licences binding on third parties:

- *Errington* v. *Errington and Woods* (1952): a contractual licence can bind third parties.
- *Binions* v. *Evans* (1972): use of a constructive trust to hold that a licence can bind a purchaser.
- *Ashburn Anstalt* v. *Arnold* (1988): these attempts disapproved. See the judgment of Fox LJ.

◼ Proprietary estoppel

The essential elements of proprietary estoppel are:

- a commitment or promise by one person (X) to another (Y);
- which X intends Y to rely on;
- and where Y's actual reliance to his detriment is reasonable in the circumstances;
- an objective test applies: thus the question is whether a promise by X can reasonably be understood as a commitment by X to Y.

The basis of the doctrine can be seen as unconscionability: would it be unconscionable for X, when Y has relied on X's promise to his detriment, to then depart from that promise?

Note that estoppel is an example of equity: this means that there is a good deal of discretion in this area and it is unwise to come to a black-and-white conclusion.

Example

X owns a piece of land and says to Y: 'You can have it as a market garden.' Y takes over the land and develops it as a market garden but the land is never conveyed to him. X later attempts to turn Y out.

Here there is no deed of conveyance but equity provides that it could be unjust to allow a person in X's position to rely on this fact, so it may be remedied by the doctrine of proprietary estoppel.

REVISION NOTE

You can see from the above example another instance of equity intervening where formalities have not been complied with. Check Chapter 1 to make sure that you remember a further instance of equity enforcing agreements where there is no deed.

Proprietary estoppel and promissory estoppel

Promissory estoppel applies in contractual relationships and essentially operates as a defence to prevent a party from going back on a promise.

Proprietary estoppel applies in property as well as contractual situations and can give rights where none existed before.

Examples of proprietary estoppel

- *Inwards* v. *Baker* (1965): a father allowed his son to build a bungalow on land owned by the father. The son was granted a licence for life.
- *Gillett* v. *Holt* (2000): even though a promise to leave property to X by will is superseded by a will which leaves the same property to Y, estoppel can still apply.

Estoppel: recent developments

The nature of proprietary estoppel has been the subject of two very important cases which you must be fully aware of for your exam.

KEY CASE

Yeoman's Row Management Ltd v. *Cobbe* [2008] UKHL 55

Concerning: estoppel – basic principles

Facts

An oral agreement between the company and Cobbe provided that a block of flats owned by the company would be demolished and Cobbe would apply for planning permission to erect houses in their place, with any excess of the proceeds over £24 million shared equally with the company. After planning permission had been obtained the company went back on the oral agreement and demanded more money. Cobbe claimed that the company was estopped from going back on the agreement.

Legal principle

Estoppel did not apply. No specific property right had been promised to Cobbe nor would it be unconscionable for the company to go back on its assurance as Cobbe knew that only a formal contract would be binding.
(Note that the actual decision was not controversial, but see below for the debate on the speech of Lord Scott.)

KEY CASE

Thorner v. *Major* [2009] UKHL 18

Concerning: estoppel – basic principles

Facts

D had worked at P's farm for no payment from 1976 onwards, and by the 1980s, hoped that he might inherit the farm. No express representation had ever been made, but D relied on various hints and remarks made by P over the years. Also in 1990 P gave D a bonus notice relating to two policies on P's life, saying 'that's for my death duties'.

Legal principle

The handing over of the bonus notice in 1990 should not be considered alone, and the evidence had demonstrated a continuing pattern of conduct by P for the remaining 15 years of his life sufficient to amount to an estoppel.

! **Don't be tempted to...**

Be careful that you discuss the underlying debate and do not just give the facts of these two cases.

Lord Scott in *Yeomans Row* v. *Cobbe* considered that proprietary estoppel should be restricted to representations of specific facts or mixed law and fact by X which stood in the way of a right claimed by Y. However, this question seemed to mean that proprietary estoppel was no different to promissory estoppel: it only applied as a defence to an action where those specific representations had been gone back on and not to enable an independent right to be asserted. Moreover, this approach would have meant that proprietary estoppel could not have applied in cases involving a promise of an inheritance as this would relate to a *future* right as in *Thorner* v. *Major* itself.

Lord Scott would have upheld the claim in *Thorner* v. *Major* on the basis of a remedial constructive trust instead as when the promise was made there was no specific property to which it could apply. The other judges however applied proprietary estoppel. See the 'Read to impress' section at the end of this chapter for references to discussion of this debate and the companion book *Law Express: Equity and Trusts* for details of the remedial constructive trust.

See also *Macdonald* v. *Frost* (2009), where the lack of any assurance was fatal to the claim.

 Make your answer stand out

Point out, especially in an essay question, that the Law Commission (Consultation Paper 186) considered whether proprietary estoppel could replace prescription as a method of acquisition of an easement (see Chapter 8) but did not favour the idea. (See paras. 4.187–4.192.) This is a useful link with another area.

Once estoppel has been established the court must decide the remedy.

KEY CASE

Jennings v. *Rice* [2003] EWCA Civ 159 (CA)

Concerning: what will be awarded to satisfy an estoppel

Facts

X worked for nearly 30 years as a gardener and odd-job man for Y. He was initially paid but then Y promised him that she would leave him her house and that he would be 'all right one day'. After this he was no longer paid. Y died intestate. X claimed either Y's whole estate (value: £1,285,000) or the value of the house (£435,000).

Legal principle

X would be awarded £200,000 as a larger sum would have been out of all proportion to what X might have charged for his services.

! Don't be tempted to...

Don't omit a discussion of how the estoppel will be satisfied. Remember that this is equity and so the court has discretion. The basic point is that any equitable right is inchoate until it crystallises in the form of an order made by the court, which gives the claimant a specific interest. The articles by Pawlowski (2002) and Thompson (2003) mentioned in the Read to Impress section at the end of this chapter will give you some pointers on how to explore this further.

Proprietary estoppel and third parties

A right by proprietary estoppel may bind a purchaser where title to the land is registered.

KEY STATUTE

Section 116, LRA 2002

This allows an equity by estoppel to be registered and can take effect from the moment it arises. Therefore, it can be protected by a notice against the title.

In addition, if the person claiming the estoppel is in occupation, under it he or she may have an overriding interest under Sch. 3, para. 2, LRA 2002.

Make your answer stand out

The elevation of estoppel rights to a proprietary right is interesting as the actual *entitlement* to which an estoppel gives rise can only be determined by the court as in *Jennings* v. *Rice*. Even so, s. 116 allows an estoppel to take effect before it has been determined by the court. Section 116 applied in *Halifax plc* v. *Curry Popeck* (2008) (see Chapter 2) where the interest of the bank was held to have arisen by proprietary estoppel.

Example

X claims to be entitled to Blackacre as Y the freehold owner had told him that he could have the land and X had erected a building on it. Y then sells the land to Z. X will then claim against Y that Y is estopped from denying X's title to the land. If the court grants the order, X will have an equitable interest which under s. 116 is taken to have arisen at the time when the facts giving rise to the estoppel took place. Thus:

- There was an estoppel at the time of the disposition by Y to Z.
- This is an equitable interest in the land.
- If X was in occupation under this interest at the time of the disposition by Y to Z (see Sch. 3 para. 2, LRA 2002).
- X can have an overriding interest which binds Z.

A really excellent way to round off an answer to a problem question on estoppel!

REVISION NOTE

Check your knowledge of registered land principles by looking through Chapter 2.

■Chapter summary: putting it all together

Test yourself

- ☐ Can you tick all the points from the **revision checklist** at the beginning of this chapter?
- ☐ Attempt the **sample question** from the beginning of this chapter using the answer guidelines below.
- ☐ Go to the **companion website** to access more revision support online, including interactive quizzes, sample questions with answer guidelines, 'you be the marker' exercises, flashcards and podcasts you can download.

Answer guidelines

See problem question at the start of the chapter. A diagram illustrating how to structure your answer is available on the companion website.

Approaching the question

This question requires a thorough knowledge of the conditions for an estoppel to apply and, for a good mark, an in-depth knowledge of the case law and recognition that, as this is equity, there are no black-and-white answers!

Important points to include

Apply conditions for an estoppel:

- ■ Representation – what Claire said?
- ■ Relied on by Emily? Emily assumed that Claire meant that she would leave her the house.
- ■ To Emily's detriment? Note that Emily drew a carer's allowance.

Cases – you must demonstrate a clear grasp of *Thorner* v. *Major*. *Gillet* v. *Holt* is also relevant.

Consider unconscionability:

- ■ If Emily succeeds then what will the remedy be?

- The court has discretion. Apply *Jennings* v. *Rice*.
- Document signed by the children – does it mean that Emily's rights bind them?
- Look at e.g. *Binions* v. *Evans*, but *Ashburn Anstalt* v. *Arnold* emphasises that *Binions* is no longer authority for the proposition that contractual licences can bind third parties.
- Her right could be registered. Apply s. 116, LRA 2002.

 Make your answer stand out

- Discussion of Lord Scott's analysis in *Thorner* v. *Major* – suggestion that a remedial constructive trust would be more appropriate. Why?
- Detailed discussion of the land registration issue angle and Sch. 3, para. 2 LRA 2002.
- Reasoning in cases such as *Ashburn* in detail.

READ TO IMPRESS

Delany and Ryan, 'Unconscionability: a unifying theme in equity?' [2008] Conv 401.

Dixon, 'Priorities under the Land Registration Act 2002' (2009) 125 LQR 401.

Hill, 'The termination of bare licences' (2001) 87 CLJ 107.

McFarlane, 'Apocalypse averted: proprietary estoppel in the House of Lords' (2009) 125 LQR 535.

Sparkes, 'Leasehold termination and contractual licences' (1988) 104 LQR 175.

Pawlowski, 'Satisfying the estoppel' (2002) 118 LQR 519.

Thompson, 'The flexibility of estoppel' [2003] Conv 225.

NOTES

NOTES

Leases

Revision checklist

Essential points you should know:

- ☐ Distinction between a lease and a licence
- ☐ Types of leases
- ☐ Legal and equitable leases
- ☐ Extent to which leases are binding on a transferee of the land
- ☐ Parties to a lease
- ☐ When a landlord can refuse consent to an assignment of a lease
- ☐ Distinction between express and implied covenants in leases
- ☐ Liability where the Landlord and Tenant (Covenants) Act 1995 applies and when it does not
- ☐ Remedies for breaches of covenants

Topic map

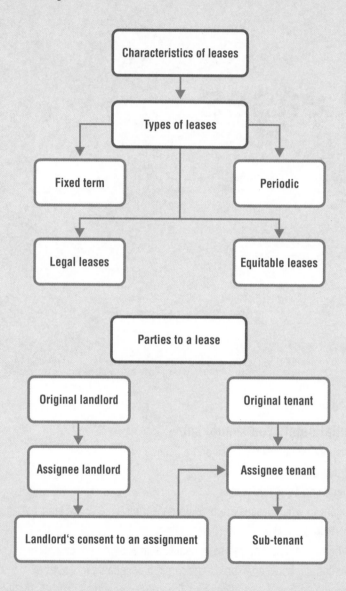

Characteristics of leases

Types of leases

Fixed term

Periodic

Legal leases

Equitable leases

Parties to a lease

Original landlord

Original tenant

Assignee landlord

Assignee tenant

Landlord's consent to an assignment

Sub-tenant

A printable version of this topic map is available from **www.pearsoned.co.uk/lawexpress**

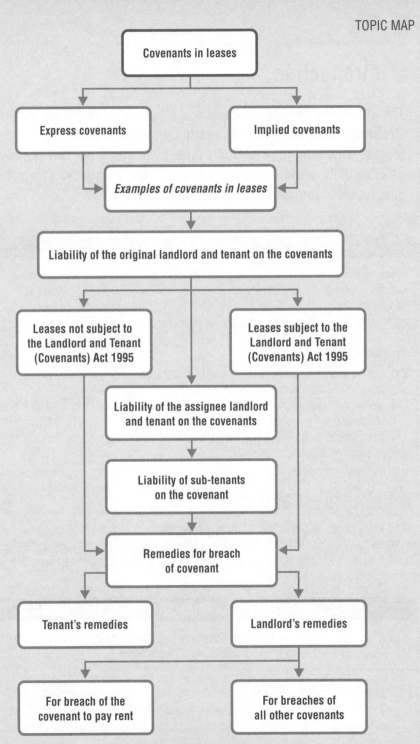

■Introduction

The difference between a lease and a licence is reasonably straightforward but it is easy to trip up on questions on types of leases: watch out for a periodic tenancy popping up! Questions on covenants contain a number of areas and as always you must adopt a clear logical approach to them.

ASSESSMENT ADVICE

Essay question A common essay question is to ask you if it matters if a lease is legal or equitable. The answer is, of course, that it does and you then need to explore this. You could get a more challenging question on the lease/licence distinction or on remedies for breach of covenants.

Problem question Examples are:

(a) the lease/licence distinction, possibly linked with what type of lease it is, assuming that it is a lease at all;

(b) whether a lease is binding on a purchaser of the freehold, this could be linked with the question in (a) above;

(c) whether the lease is binding on a third party;

(d) liability for breach of covenants.

■Sample question

Could you answer this question? Below is a typical problem question that could arise on this topic. Guidelines on answering the question are included at the end of this chapter, while a sample essay question and guidance on tackling it can be found on the companion website.

PROBLEM QUESTION

Fiona has just purchased 155 High Street Hanbury, a freehold registered property, consisting of a house and an adjoining office, from Terry.

(a) The top floor of the house is occupied by Ted under an agreement made two years ago where he is allowed to stay for five years paying rent at £300 a quarter. The agreement is unsigned and it provides that the owner of the house agrees to clean Ted's premises and retains a duplicate key to enable the owner to enter in order to do this. Ted tells Fiona that Terry never cleaned the premises and that Ted never wanted him to do so. Fiona wishes to evict Ted.

(b) The office is occupied by Josephine under a seven-year legal lease granted by Terry last year at a rent of £6,000 a year, payable quarterly. The lease contains the following covenants:

(i) Josephine will keep the premises in good repair.

(ii) The permitted use of the premises is a high-class retail shop.

(iii) The lease cannot be assigned without the consent of the landlord.

(iv) In the event of any breach of covenant, the landlord may forfeit the lease.

Josephine now wishes to assign the lease to Eileen, who wishes to open a travel agency. In addition, Josephine's rent for the previous year has not been paid and Fiona has discovered that the premises have not been kept in repair.

Advise Fiona on her rights and obligations.

◼ Characteristics of a lease

KEY DEFINITIONS: Lease and licence

A **lease** is an estate in the land which, therefore, gives a proprietary interest in the land. It must be distinguished from a **licence** which only gives a personal right in the land. Although the fact that licences only create personal interests has proved controversial in the past, it is the law today.

REVISION NOTE

Go to Chapters 1 and 5 and revise leases as proprietary interests and licences as personal interests.

Keep in mind two vital consequences of the right being a lease and not a licence:

1 It can bind third parties, e.g. purchasers of the freehold.
2 The holder of a lease has security of tenure created by statute but a licensee has not.

Note terminology: the parties to a lease are the **landlord** and the **tenant**, but they are legally the **lessor** (landlord) and the **lessee** (tenant).

You will not be required to know the details of the statutory protection given to tenants in a land law exam unless your syllabus expressly includes landlord and tenant law.

The essential characteristics of a lease

Street v. *Mountford* **[1985] 2 All ER 289 (HL)**

Concerning: the essential characteristics of a lease

Facts

Under what was described as a licence agreement, X was given exclusive possession of furnished rooms at a rent. She had signed a statement at the end of the agreement that this was not intended to give rise to a tenancy under the Rent Acts. It was held that in fact she did have a tenancy.

Legal principle

A lease must have three characteristics:

1 exclusive possession;
2 for a fixed or periodic term;
3 at a rent.

If so, there will be a tenancy, unless there are exceptional circumstances which make it a licence.

The fact that the agreement is described as a licence does not prevent it from being a lease if the above characteristics are present. The only intention of the parties which is relevant is the intention to grant exclusive possession.

Note that there is no absolute principle of no rent, no lease. See *Ashburn Anstalt* v. *Arnold* (1989).

There have been many cases which have applied the principles in *Street* v. *Mountford.*

KEY CASE

Antoniades v. *Villiers* [1988] 3 All ER 1058 (HL)

Concerning: whether 'separate' licence agreements were in fact a lease

Facts

A couple entered into two separate but identical agreements under which they were given the right to occupy rooms and each had separate responsibility for payment of half the rent. The agreement provided that they were to use the rooms either in common with the owner or with other licensees permitted by him.

Legal principle

Despite the attempt to make this look like two separate licence agreements, it was, in fact, a lease. A vital point was that they had the choice of either two single beds or one double bed. They chose a double bed and so clearly they intended to occupy the rooms jointly.

Compare this case with *AG Securities* v. *Vaughan* (1988).

Note a common point for exam questions: the landlord retains a set of keys. In *Aslan* v. *Murphy* (1990) it was held that this by itself did not prevent a lease.

 Make your answer stand out

In *Bruton* v. *London and Quadrant Housing Trust* (1999) the HL indicated that a lease could create purely personal rights between the parties and this 'personal' tenancy is binding on the immediate landlord but not on anyone with a superior title. Look at this case carefully and read Pawlowski (2002) and Hinjosa (2005).

The rule that a lease must be for a term certain is illustrated by *Prudential Assurance v. London Residuary Body* (1992): lease granted until a road required for road widening invalid.

Leases are classified by the length of time they last for and the main types to learn for an exam are:

- leases for a fixed term;
- periodic tenancies.

You also need to know:

KEY DEFINITION: Tenancy at will

The tenant, with the owner's consent, occupies land at the will of the owner, who, therefore, may terminate it at any time. The tenant has no security of tenure and is really in no better position than a licensee except that as a tenant there is a right to exclusive possession.

KEY DEFINITION: Tenant at sufferance

The tenant, after the expiry of the lease, continues in possession without the consent of the landlord (remember that a tenant at will does have consent). A tenant at sufferance has no real tenancy and cannot even sue another for trespass (*Schwartz* v. *Zamrl* (1968)).

Periodic tenancies often arise in exam questions and it is vital to be able to recognise them: they arise from payment of rent at periodic intervals. There are two types:

1 *Express periodic tenancies*, e.g. where a tenancy is granted but the precise length of it is not declared.
2 *Implied periodic tenancies.* These are probably more likely in an exam question as they can be linked with a question where the formalities for the creation of an express legal or equitable lease were not observed.

Example

X agrees by a written agreement to let a flat to Y. The agreement is signed by Y but not by X. However, Y goes into possession and pays rent monthly.

This is not a legal lease as it is not by deed nor is it a valid equitable lease as it does not satisfy the requirements of s. 2 of the Law of Property (Miscellaneous Provisions) Act 1989 (see below and Chapter 1).

Y may claim a monthly periodic tenancy based on payment of rent. Do point out that there is only a presumption that there is a tenancy – see the CA in *Javad* v. *Mohammad Aqil* (1991) but in the above facts it is highly likely that one would be implied.

Another example of a periodic tenancy is where there is no agreement at all and the 'tenant' is just allowed into possession and then pays rent at regular intervals. The payment of rent converts what is just a tenancy at will into a periodic tenancy.

Periodic tenancies are likely to be legal (not exceeding three years – see below) and will not require registration (not exceeding seven years – see below and Chapter 1).

REVISION NOTE

Check the requirements for legal and equitable leases.

■ Types of leases

Legal leases

A lease will be legal if created by deed, but there is an important exception:

REVISION NOTE

Check that you are familiar with what a deed is and the requirements for its creation – see Chapter 1.

KEY STATUTE

Section 54(2), LPA 1925

A lease not exceeding three years can be legal without any formalities (even oral) if:

- in possession;
- best rent – commercial rent;
- no fine – no premium.

EXAM TIP

Watch for periodic tenancies (above) in the exam: these will be legal as the length of the lease will be less than three years.

Equitable leases

A lease can be equitable under the principle in *Walsh* v. *Lonsdale* (1882) as an agreement for a lease but it must satisfy the three requirements for a valid agreement set out in s. 2 of the Law of Property (Miscellaneous Provisions) Act 1989.

REVISION NOTE

Check Chapter 1 to make sure that you understand and can apply these requirements.

KEY CASE

Walsh v. *Lonsdale* [1882] 21 Ch D 9 (HC)

Concerning: the creation of equitable leases

Facts

A lease was granted but not by deed. Thus it was only equitable – an agreement for a lease can be enforced by equity on the basis of the maxim that 'equity looks on that as done which ought to be done', i.e. if a person has agreed to grant a lease then he ought to do so and, as far as possible, equity will assume that he has done so.

Legal principle

An agreement for a lease can create a valid equitable lease.

! Don't be tempted to...

Don't rush into answering a problem question on types of leases. Take your time and think through a logical approach.

Try this:

- How long is the lease for? If not exceeding three years, it can be legal without formalities, provided that s. 54(2), LPA is satisfied.
- If it exceeds three years, was it created by deed? If so, it is legal (and can also be an overriding interest if it does not exceed seven years – see below).
- If there is no deed, then is there an agreement for a lease which satisfies s. 2 of the Law of Property (Miscellaneous Provisions) Act 1989? If so, lease will be equitable.
- If tenant pays rent regularly, then can have a periodic tenancy – legal and likely to be overriding as less than seven years.

Comparison between legal and equitable leases

A very common essay question asks you if there are any differences between legal and equitable leases.

Legal leases	Equitable leases
Created by deed except for leases not exceeding three years	Created by agreement which satisfies s. 2, Law of Property (Miscellaneous Provisions) Act 1989
Not granted at the discretion of the court	Granted at the discretion of the court – equitable remedies are discretionary
Tenant under a legal lease can claim implied easements under s. 62(1), LPA 1925	Tenant under an equitable lease cannot claim implied easements under s. 62(1), LPA 1925 – equitable lease is not a conveyance

In addition, there are different rules on whether legal and equitable leases can bind third parties – see below.

REVISION NOTE

Check Chapter 8 and make sure that you understand and can apply the rule on creation of easements in s. 62(1), LPA 1925.

■ Leases and third parties

REVISION NOTE

This was dealt with in Chapter 2, and you should check your knowledge of registered land and unregistered land now.

Summary: registered and unregistered land (leases)

Registered land	Unregistered land
Legal leases for over seven years are registrable dispositions	Legal leases are binding on all third parties
Legal leases for less than this period are overriding interests	
Equitable leases should be registered as estate contracts but, if they are not and if the leaseholder is in actual occupation, they may have an overriding interest under Sch. 3, para. 2 of the LRA 2002	Equitable leases need to be protected on the register of land charges as estate contracts: Class C(iv)

REVISION NOTE

Check registered land and land charges in Chapter 2.

EXAM TIP

When you get a problem question on leases, check the *length* of the leases to see:

- What formalities are needed – vital length is not exceeding three years.
- If the lease is legal, does it need to be substantively registered? – vital length is not exceeding seven years.

So, think three years and then seven years!

■ Parties to a lease

The area covered by this chapter often forms a problem question in an exam. The situation can be set out in the following diagram.

Keep this diagram in mind when studying this chapter, and if you get an exam question on this area then make a diagram like this to show who the parties are and their positions.

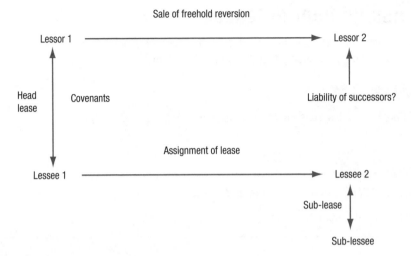

KEY DEFINITION: Parties to a lease

Note the following terms in the above diagram:

- **Lessor**: grantor of the lease.

- **Lessee**: grantee of the lease.

- **Headlease**: lease granted by the lessor to the lessee as distinct from a sub-lease.

- **Freehold reversion**: the rights retained by the lessor on the grant of a lease.

- **Assignment**: disposition of the lessee's interest to the assignee who then takes over the assignor's interest in the land.

- **Underlease/sub-lease**: creation of a subsidiary estate out of the lessee's estate.

EXAM TIP

When you get a problem question on leases, before you do anything else, you must ask two questions:

1 Is the lease legal or equitable?
2 What date was it granted? If it was on or after 1 January 1996, your answer will differ from one if it was before this date as the Landlord and Tenant (Covenants) Act 1995 applies. The actual changes are explained below.

Assignment of leases

Check whether the lease either prohibits an assignment altogether or (more likely) allows assignment providing that the landlord consents.

> **EXAM TIP**
>
> Be prepared for a question asking you to discuss a refusal of consent.

> **KEY STATUTE**
>
> **Section 19(1), Landlord and Tenant Act 1927**
>
> The landlord must not withhold consent unreasonably.

> **KEY CASE**
>
> *International Drilling Fluids Ltd v. Louisville Investments Ltd* [1986] All ER 321 (HC)
>
> *Concerning: refusal by landlord of consent to an assignment of a lease*
>
> **Legal principle**
>
> The landlord is entitled to be protected from having the premises used or occupied in an undesirable way by an undesirable assignee (or tenant), but consent to an assignment cannot be refused on grounds which have nothing to do with the relationship of landlord and tenant. So, a personal dislike would not be enough.

> **KEY STATUTE**
>
> **Section 1(3) and 1(6), Landlord and Tenant Act 1988**
>
> Section 1(3): if the tenant asks for consent in writing, the landlord must give or refuse consent in writing and must do this in a reasonable time.
>
> Section 1(6): it is for the landlord to prove that:
>
> ■ a refusal of consent was reasonable;
>
> ■ consent was given or withheld in a reasonable time;
>
> ■ if conditions were imposed, that they were reasonable.

Examples of where a refusal of consent would be reasonable:

- Where the landlord reasonably believes that a proposed assignment would lead to a breach of covenant in the lease – see the HL in *Ashworth Frazer Ltd* v. *Gloucester City Council* (2001).

- The assignee tenant's references were unsatisfactory.

- The financial standing of the assignee is unsatisfactory.

In *Kened Ltd and Den Norske Bank plc* v. *Connie Investments Ltd* (1997), Millett LJ said that the essential question is: 'Has it been shown that no reasonable landlord would have withheld consent?'

Note this point in relation to leases granted on or after 1 January 1996.

KEY STATUTE

Section 19(1A), Landlord and Tenant Act 1927, (added by s. 22, Landlord and Tenant (Covenants) Act 1995)

Landlord and tenant of a non-residential lease may agree in the lease what circumstances will justify the landlord in withholding consent.

Note that the above provision is relevant to the assignor tenant's continuing liability for breach of the covenants – see below.

Covenants in leases

Distinguish between:

- express covenants, i.e. actually contained in the lease;
- implied covenants, i.e. implied by law.

KEY DEFINITION: Covenants

Promises in a deed.

Even where the lease is equitable (i.e. no deed) it is usual to talk of covenants.

EXAM TIP

Typical examples of covenants in an exam question are: repairing, payment of rent, that the tenant will only use the premises for certain purposes. Exam questions will normally set these out as express covenants.

Implied covenants are implied in the lease unless excluded – good ones to remember for the exam are:

- *Tenant's covenant to repair.* If the premises are in disrepair at the start of the lease then if the tenant covenants to 'keep them in repair' this means that he must put them in repair at his expense – *Payne* v. *Haine* (1847).

- *Landlord's covenant for quiet enjoyment.* I.e. that the tenant will not be disturbed by third-party rights and acts of the landlord which disturb possession, e.g. burst water pipes causing water to flow into the premises. If this covenant is broken, there could also be liability for breach of s. 1(3) of the Protection from Eviction Act 1977 – unlawful harassment.

! Don't be tempted to...

A common exam question asks you about noise: this is a trap! Note Kekewich LJ in *Jenkins* v. *Jackson* (1888), who observed that this covenant does not mean 'undisturbed by noise'. You will win marks here if you mention the judgments in *Southwark LBC* v. *Mills* (2001), where the covenant was *not* broken by failure of the landlord to provide soundproofing in flats.

- *Landlord's covenants not to derogate from his grant.* I.e. not frustrate the purposes for which the premises were let such as interfere with a right to light. The covenant does not prevent the landlord setting up a competing business – *Port* v. *Griffith* (1938).

✓ Make your answer stand out

Ask if *Port* v. *Griffith* would apply if the premises were to be let for a highly specialised purpose.

- *Tenant's covenant not to commit waste.* This means that 'the tenant must take proper care of the place' (Denning LJ in *Warren* v. *Keen* (1954)).

We will come to the remedies for breaches of covenants a little later in this chapter.

Liability of the original landlord and tenant on the covenants

The original landlord and tenant are of course liable on the covenants while they are the actual landlord and tenant. When the freehold and the leasehold are assigned they may continue to be liable. This depends on whether the Landlord and Tenant (Covenants) Act 1995 applies. The Act applies to *all* leases granted on or after 1 January 1996 which by s. 1(1) are referred to as 'new tenancies'. Pre-1 January 1996 tenancies are referred to as 'other tenancies'.

Note that by s. 28(1) a 'new tenancy' includes an *agreement* for a tenancy, i.e. an equitable lease.

■ If the legal (not equitable) lease was granted before 1 January 1996, both landlord and tenant remain liable on the covenants for the whole term of the lease even if they are no longer parties, i.e. the tenant has assigned the lease and the landlord has sold the freehold reversion. But note s. 17 Landlord and Tenants (Covenants) Act 1995.

■ If the lease was granted on or after 1 January 1996, then the Landlord and Tenant (Covenants) Act 1995 applies to legal and equitable leases.

Note that all the references to sections below are to sections of this Act.

KEY STATUTE

Section 5, Landlord and Tenant (Covenants) Act 1995

The tenant on assigning the lease is released from his covenants and ceases to be entitled to the benefit of the landlord covenants.

■ However, the landlord may, as a condition of agreeing to the assignment, require the tenant to enter into an authorised guarantee agreement (AGA) (s. 16) guaranteeing that the incoming tenant will perform the covenants.

Example

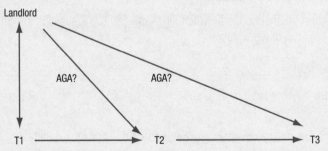

When the landlord gives consent to the assignment from T1 to T2, he can require T1 to enter an AGA under which T1 guarantees T2's liabilities under the lease. When T2 assigns to T3, the landlord may require T2 to enter into an AGA, but when the assignment is complete, T1's liability ends. This is a common exam point.

Section 6, Landlord and Tenant (Covenants) Act 1995

The landlord may, on selling the freehold reversion, be released from liability on his covenants. The procedure is set out in s. 8.

EXAM TIP

Students often think that the date for deciding if the Landlord and Tenant (Covenants) Act 1995 applies is the date of the assignment of the lease. It is not. It is the date when the lease was originally granted.

Liability of the assignee landlord and tenant on the covenants

Once again, it is necessary to distinguish between pre-1 January 1996 and post-1 January 1996 leases:

Pre-1 January 1996 leases

In this situation the distinction between legal and equitable leases is important as covenants only run in legal leases.

EXAM TIP

Check if the lease is legal or equitable.

Tenant 2 is liable on the covenants, provided that two tests are satisfied:

1 There is 'privity of estate' between the landlord and the tenant. This originally meant the parties holding the legal estate created by the original lease, i.e. the original landlord and tenant. However, this principle has now been extended to assignee tenants (by common law) and assignee landlords (s. 141, LPA 1925 – below).

2 The covenants 'touch and concern the land' (*Spencer's Case* (1582)), e.g. covenants to pay the rent, user covenants, but not a covenant giving the tenant the right to purchase the freehold nor personal covenants.

KEY CASE

Thomas v. *Hayward* **(1869) LR 4 Ex 311**

Concerning: whether a covenant 'touches and concerns the land'

Facts

The landlord of a public house covenanted that he would not open another 'beer or spirit house' within half a mile of the premises.

Legal principle

This did not bind an assignee tenant as it did not refer to anything to be done or not done on the premises.

Landlord 2 is liable to T2 under s. 142, LPA 1925 and can enforce covenants which 'have reference to the subject matter of the lease' (s. 141, LPA 1925). This term means fundamentally the same as the common law term 'touch and concern' and is also a useful guide in cases involving tenant's covenants.

Post-1 January 1996 leases

The rules apply to both legal and equitable leases as we saw above.

KEY STATUTE

Section 3, Landlord and Tenant (Covenants) Act 1995

'The benefit of all landlord and tenant covenants of a tenancy … shall in accordance with this section pass on an assignment of the whole or any part of the premises or of the reversion of them.'

Both incoming landlords and tenants are bound by covenants unless they are not landlord and tenant covenants, i.e. they are 'personal in character'. This is very similar to the old 'touch and concern' test.

Note that a question may involve breach by, for instance, a landlord of a covenant to repair and a refusal of the tenant in consequence to pay rent. Breach by one party does not excuse breach by the other and so the tenant is still liable to pay rent.

> **! Don't be tempted to...**
>
> Make sure that you are clear about the liability of sub-tenants on a covenant in a lease. Remember these three points:
>
> 1 There is no privity of estate between the landlord under the headlease and the subtenant (ST), i.e. the landlord is not a party to the sub-lease. This means that the landlord and the ST cannot directly enforce covenants against each other.
> 2 The landlord can, as an exception to the above rule, enforce a restrictive covenant which is negative by an injunction against ST.
> 3 The landlord can sue the tenant under the headlease for a breach of covenant committed by the sub-tenant and so claim to forfeit the lease – see below.

Example

There are two covenants in a lease:

(a) to repair the premises;
(b) not to use the premises for any purpose other than a high-class grocer's shop.

T has sub-let to ST. L can enforce covenant (b) against ST but can only enforce covenant (a) against T.

REVISION NOTE

Check Chapter 7 for the rules on restrictive covenants.

■ Remedies for breach of covenants
Tenant's remedies

Exam questions usually ask you about breaches of covenant by the tenant and so you need to concentrate on the landlord's remedies. In brief, the tenant's remedies are:

- damages, e.g. for breach of covenant by the landlord to repair;

- repudiation of the lease – possibly linked to a claim for damages;

- specific performance, e.g. *Posner* v. *Scott-Lewis* (1986) – granted in respect of an obligation to employ a resident porter at a block of flats;

- appointment of a receiver, e.g. to make repairs.

Landlord's remedies

For breach of the covenant to pay rent

- Action for arrears of rent. Limited to six years' arrears, s. 19, Limitation Act 1980.
- Forfeiture proceedings. This is the remedy which an exam question is most likely to ask you to deal with and you should approach it as shown in the diagram.

Note: The remedy of distress was abolished by the Tribunals, Courts and Enforcement Act 2007. There is a replacement remedy for commercial leases.

For breaches of all other covenants

- Damages, e.g. for breach of the tenant's covenant to repair.
- Injunction, e.g. to prevent breaches of covenants.
- Forfeiture. Once again, an exam question may require you to deal with this in detail. Note carefully the differences in forfeiture here from forfeiture for non-payment of rent.

 Make your answer stand out

Exam questions often ask if a particular breach can be remedied.

The main case to mention here is *Expert Clothing Service and Sales Ltd* v. *Hillgate House Ltd* (1986).

You may get a question where the tenant's use of the premises has cast a stigma over the premises, e.g. *Rugby School* v. *Tannahill* (1935): use of premises for prostitution. Even if the use has ceased, the stigma may remain and so the breach cannot be remedied in a reasonable time.

Note: Even if forfeiture proceedings succeed, a court order is still needed to evict a residential occupier – s. 3(1), Protection from Eviction Act 1977. Occupier means any person lawfully residing in the premises and so includes licensees (ss. 3(2A) and (2B)).

REVISION NOTE

Check Chapter 5 alongside this chapter to make sure that you are clear on the idea of a licensee and the distinction between a licence and a lease.

EXAM TIP

Point out the possible relevance of the ECHR in an eviction situation. Check Chapter 1 for details.

Make your answer stand out

The law on the landlord's remedies has been reconsidered by the Law Commission (2004) which proposed a new 'termination scheme' with no distinction between termination for non-payment of rent and for other reasons. A reference to their proposals will gain you extra marks.

Forfeiture for non-payment of rent

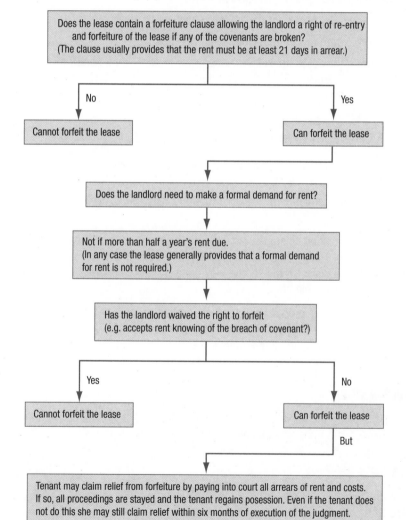

Forfeiture for other breaches

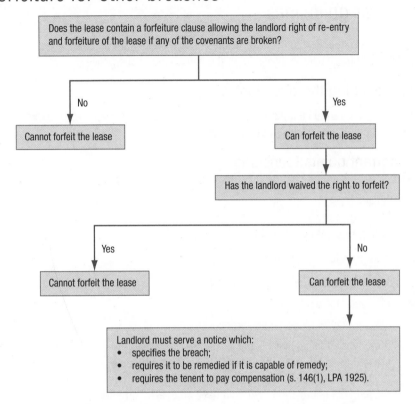

■ **Chapter summary**: putting it all together

Test yourself

- ☐ Can you tick all the points from the **revision checklist** at the beginning of this chapter?
- ☐ Attempt the **sample question** from the beginning of this chapter using the answer guidelines below.
- ☐ Go to the **companion website** to access more revision support online, including interactive quizzes, sample questions with answer guidelines, 'you be the marker' exercises, flashcards and podcasts you can download.

Answer guidelines

See problem question at the start of the chapter. A diagram illustrating how to structure your answer is available on the companion website.

Approaching the question

This question ranges across the whole area of Chapter 6 and contains many different points. An excellent opportunity to score a really good mark!

Important points to include

(a) Lease or licence? Look at the three tests:

1 Exclusive possession?
2 Payment of rent?
3 Intention to create relationship of landlord and tenant?

If it could be a lease, is it for a definite term?

Could be a lease or a licence, so consider:

■ If a licence, not binding on Fiona.

■ If a lease, may bind Fiona, but first check:

 – What type of lease is it? Legal leases for more than three years should be created by deed (s. 54(2), LPA 1925). Is it an equitable lease? Apply *Walsh* v. *Lonsdale* and s. 2, Law of Property (Miscellaneous Provisions) Act 1989. As Ted is in occupation, he could have an overriding interest.

 – If equitable, does it bind Fiona? Title is registered, so agreement could have been registered as an estate contract but does not seem to have been.

 – May be a periodical quarterly lease as rent has been paid. If so, will count as an overriding interest (lease for less than seven years) and will bind Fiona.

(b) Lease was entered into after 1 January 1996, so the Landlord and Tenant (Covenants) Act 1996 will apply – counts as a 'new tenancy'.

Breach of repair and use covenant. Fiona may sue – s. 141, LPA 1925.

Assignment of lease: s. 19, Landlord and Tenant Act 1927 – can consent be withheld? Yes, as Eileen's proposed use is in breach of covenant.

Remedies of Fiona:

■ damages;

■ forfeiture – lease has forfeiture clause – procedure – apply s. 146, LPA 1925 – can breaches be remedied? Discuss cases.

Make your answer stand out

- Refer to the Law Commission's proposals in this area.
- If there is an overriding interest, discuss whether it is actually binding by referring to Sch. 3, para. 2 of the LRA 2002 – check Chapter 2.

READ TO IMPRESS

Bright, 'Leases, exclusive possession and estates' (2000) 116 LQR 7.

Bright, 'Avoiding tenancy legislation: sham and contracting out revisited' (2002) CLJ 146.

Hinjosa, 'On property, leases, licences, horses and carts: revisiting Bruton v. Quadrant Housing Trust' [2005] Conv 114.

Law Commission Consultation Paper 174, 'Termination of tenancies for tenant default' (2004).

Pawlowski, 'Occupational rights in leasehold law: time for rationalisation?' [2002] Conv 550.

NOTES

NOTES

Covenants affecting freehold land

7

Revision checklist

Essential points you should know:

- [ ] Positive and negative covenants
- [ ] Liability of the original covenantor
- [ ] When s. 56(1) of the LPA 1925 could apply
- [ ] Rules on when the benefit of a restrictive covenant may run
- [ ] Rules on when the burden of a restrictive covenant may run at common law
- [ ] The remedies for breach of a restrictive covenant
- [ ] Law Commission proposals for reform

■ Topic map

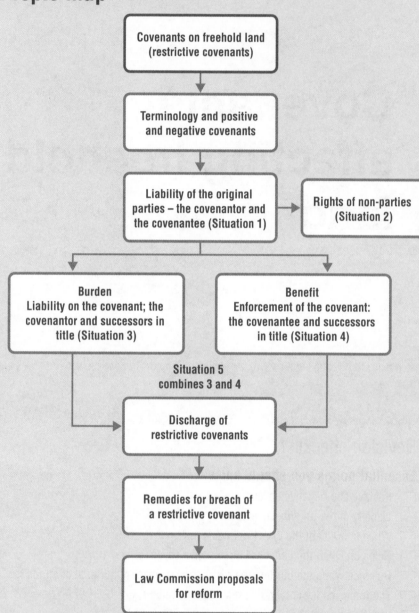

A printable version of this topic map is available from **www.pearsoned.co.uk/lawexpress**

■Introduction

John owns a large area of land. He sells part of it (Blackacre) to Rosemary but keeps Whiteacre on which he has a house. As he is still going to live nearby, he wants to retain some control over the use that can be made of it. Therefore, he imposes restrictions in the transfer to Rosemary which are known as *restrictive covenants*. The rules are not complex in themselves: the problem is seeing how they relate to each other. Make sure that you can do this. In addition in any answer you will gain extra marks by mentioning the proposals for reform contained in the Law Commission Consultation Paper 186 and which are summarised at the end of this chapter.

ASSESSMENT ADVICE

Essay questions A typical essay will ask you to discuss whether the present law needs reforming. To answer this you need:

■ A thorough knowledge of problem areas in the current law;

■ A knowledge of the proposals for reform.

An alternative is a straightforward question asking you to outline the present rules.

Problem questions All examination problem questions in this area usually begin with the scenario mentioned in the introduction above and there are two fundamental questions: who is bound by the restrictive covenant, and who can enforce it? Once you have mastered this scenario, the good news is that virtually all restrictive covenant questions follow this pattern – there are unlikely to be many variations.

Remember this checklist:

■ Who is the covenantor and who is the covenantee?

■ Which covenants are positive and which are negative?

■ Is title to the land registered or unregistered?

■ Sample question

Could you answer this question? Below is a typical problem question that could arise on this topic. Guidelines on answering the question are included at the end of the chapter, while a sample essay question and guidance on tackling it can be found on the companion website.

PROBLEM QUESTION

John owns a large area of land. He sells part of it (Blackacre) to Rosemary but keeps Whiteacre on which he has a house. As he is still going to live nearby, he wants to retain some control over the use that can be made of Blackacre. Therefore, he imposes restrictions in the transfer to Rosemary which are known as restrictive covenants. These are:

(a) that no business shall be carried on at Blackacre;

(b) that all fences must be kept in repair;

(c) that the owner of Blackacre shall contribute to the maintenance of the sewers which serve both Blackacre and Whiteacre.

These covenants are expressed to be for the benefit of Blackacre.

Rosemary subsequently sells Blackacre to Aidan, and John sells Whiteacre to Eileen. Aidan has decided to run his accountancy business from Blackacre and is seeking planning permission from the local authority to enable him to do this. He has failed to repair the fences and he refuses to contribute to the maintenance of the sewers.

Advise Eileen on any action which she may take against Aidan to enforce the covenants. Title to both Blackacre and Whiteacre is registered.

Note: to help you to understand this area, we will use examples from this question in the chapter.

■ Covenants on freehold land (definitions)
Covenants on freehold land

Covenants are promises contained in deeds and, as a transfer of the freehold title to land must be by deed (s. 52(1), LPA 1925), Rosemary's promises to John in the above scenario are called covenants.

Restrictive covenants

A restrictive covenant is a type of covenant which restricts the use of land (e.g. it provides that the land shall not be built on). The word 'restrictive' in this topic is, in fact, misleading, although the term will be used in this chapter as it is so commonly used.

Positive and negative covenants

Covenants on land are of two types: positive and negative.

> **KEY DEFINITION: Negative covenant**
>
> One which restricts the use to which the land may be put. The simplest test for distinguishing between positive and negative covenants is to ask if performance of them requires expenditure of money.

> **EXAM TIP**
>
> Knowing the distinction between positive and negative covenants is vital to answering a question on this area.

Covenants which 'touch and concern the land' and personal covenants

The former phrase has been met before in Chapter 6 on leases and it means that the covenant must benefit the land itself. The real point is that the covenant must not be personal, e.g. 'to do X's shopping for him'. The importance of this distinction will become clear in situation three.

The parties involved

The person who agrees to the covenant is the *covenantor* and the person with whom the agreement is made is the *covenantee*. The covenantor will be usually be the buyer of the land because the seller will have required the buyer to agree to the covenants as a condition of the sale. In the above question Rosemary is the covenantor and John is the covenantee.

> **EXAM TIP**
>
> Your first step in answering a problem question on covenants should always be to identify the covenantor and covenantee.

Benefit and burden

Land to which the covenant applies is *burdened* by the covenant and this will be land owned by the *covenantor*. Land owned by the *covenantee* is *benefited* by the covenant. Thus in the above question Blackacre, owned by Rosemary, is the burdened land and Whiteacre owned by John is the benefited land.

Registered and unregistered title to land

REVISION NOTE

Go back to Chapter 2 and check that you know how restrictive covenants fit into the scheme of registered and unregistered land.

Note that this chapter only deals with covenants on freehold land; leasehold covenants are dealt with in Chapter 6.

Exam questions will be most unlikely to mix up freehold and leasehold covenants. In short, the message is not to worry about leasehold covenants for now!

There are *five basic situations* that occur with restrictive covenants, and problems in an examination will revolve around these. The figure below illustrates these (note: situation two is not shown here).

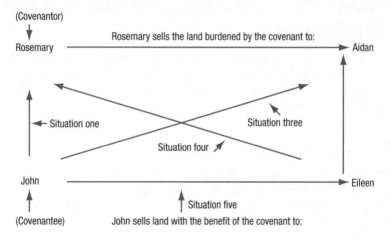

▮ Situation one: liability of the original parties – the covenantor and the covenantee

John is the original covenantee and Rosemary is the original covenantor. Rosemary is in breach of the covenants.

Rosemary

Rosemary has failed to keep the fences in repair and is now running a guest house from the premises

John

(a) The original parties can claim against each other on the covenant, so John (the covenantee) can claim against (Rosemary) (the covenantor).

In the above situation, John can sue Rosemary on the covenants. As between the original parties, all covenants are binding, which means that this basic rule applies to all covenants.

When the rights of subsequent parties are involved, the law distinguishes between these different types of covenants.

(b) The original covenantor may continue to be liable on the covenant even though he/she is no longer the owner of the land. This rule is not only one of common law but is also implied by:

KEY STATUTE

Section 79(1), LPA 1925

This provides that a covenant relating to any land of the covenantor shall be deemed to be made 'on behalf of himself and his successors in title'.

This means that the covenant can not only be binding on successors in title but that the original covenantor is liable for any breaches by successors in title. However, the rule in s. 79(1) will not apply if the covenant provides that the liability of the original covenantor is to cease when he/she sells the land.

If Rosemary sells Blackacre to Aidan, she needs to take a covenant from Aidan that he will comply with the covenants. Then, if Aidan does breach them and Rosemary is sued by John, she can sue Aidan. When Aidan sells he should take a similar covenant from his buyer and so liability moves down the line with a chain of covenants, known as *indemnity covenants*.

■ Situation two: rights of non-parties

This is the same scenario as situation one but with an addition:

Rosemary enters into the standard covenants with John but also enters into the same covenants with 'the owners of land adjacent to the land conveyed'. This means that she has covenanted with the owners of land (Greensleaves) adjacent to John's land (Whiteacre), in this case Albert.

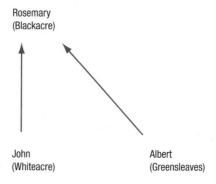

The right of Albert to enforce the covenant is contained in s. 56(1) of the LPA 1925.

KEY STATUTE

Section 56(1), LPA 1925

'A person may take ... the benefit of any condition, right of entry, covenant or agreement over or respecting land or other property, although he may not be named as a party to the conveyance or other instrument.'

Thus in our scenario – where the provision regarding adjacent landowners is spelled out in the covenant – s. 56(1) would allow adjacent owners of land to sue. If there wasn't such a clause in our scenario, s. 56(1) would not apply.

EXAM TIP

In any exam question ask if the person seeking to enforce the benefit of the covenant was in existence at the time the covenant was made. If the answer is yes, then he or she may be able to enforce the covenant subject to the test below.

See *Re Ecclesiastical Commissioners Conveyance* (1936).

Neuberger J in *Amsprop Trading Ltd* v. *Harris Distribution Ltd* (1997): 'The true aim of section 56 seems to be not to allow a third party to sue on a contract merely because it is for his benefit; *the contract must purport to be made with him*', i.e. does the covenantor actually promise the covenantee that owners of adjacent land will benefit?

KEY STATUTE

Section 1, Contracts (Rights of Third Parties) Act 1999

Section 1 enables a person who is not a party to a contract to take the benefit of a contractual term which purports to confer a benefit on him.

This Act covers the whole of the law of contract, not just this area; but in this area this Act and s. 56(1) of the LPA overlap.

This wording clearly applies to our situation as the covenant is contained in a contract and it confers a benefit on third parties, i.e. Albert as an adjoining landowner. Thus, it can be seen how s. 56(1) of the LPA and this Act overlap, and a good answer would explain that either could be used.

It is possible to have wording which would allow Albert to claim under the Contracts (Rights of Third Parties) Act 1999 but not under s. 56(1): 'this covenant is entered into with the owners of all land adjoining Whiteacre', rather than the owners of land 'now or formerly forming part of Whiteacre'. It could be argued that this could include Albert if he acquired Greensleaves *after* Rosemary entered into covenants.

EXAM TIP

Look carefully at the exact wording of the covenant and see to whom it applies.

◾ Situation three: liability on the covenant – the covenantor and successors in title

Common law and equity

Equity goes further than the common law in allowing the enforcement of covenants between successors in title of the original parties. The common law and equitable rules do not overlap and so the fact that they are mutually exclusive means that examination answers must carefully distinguish between them.

Situation three in detail

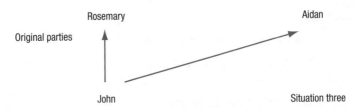

The starting position is scenario one, with Rosemary and John as the original covenantor and covenantee. However, Rosemary now sells Blackacre to Aidan. John remains the owner of Whiteacre. Assume that Aidan is in breach of all the covenants. Can John bring an action against Aidan?

This section will consider in each case whether the *burden* of the covenant has passed to Aidan.

The answers are different in each case but initially we can leave covenant (c) till later and deal with (a) and (b).

Covenants (a) and (b)

The first thing that you should do with this situation is consider which of the covenants are *positive* and which are *negative*. The covenant in (a) is negative and in (b) is positive.

The distinction between positive and negative covenants is vital because positive covenants generally only bind the original covenantor, i.e. Rosemary in the above question, and not subsequent parties, i.e. Aidan. Equity takes a different view and generally negative covenants can bind subsequent parties.

The rules on positive covenants in more detail

The common law rule on positive covenants was established in *Austerberry* v. *Oldham Corporation* (1885) where it was held that at common law positive covenants do not bind subsequent owners of land (followed in *Rhone* v. *Stephens* (1994)). Applied to situation three, this means that positive covenant (b) to keep all fences in repair *is not* binding on Aidan.

The rules on negative covenants in more detail

Equity takes a different view on *negative* covenants, as established in the following case:

KEY CASE

Tulk v. *Moxhay* (1848) Ph 774 (CA)

Concerning: negative covenants – binding on subsequent owners of land

Facts

There was a covenant not to build on land in the middle of Leicester Square in London.

Legal principle

It was held that it was binding on a subsequent purchaser of that land and so restrictive covenants take effect as an equitable interest in land.

Applied to our situation, and provided that the conditions set out below are satisfied, the negative covenant (a) not to carry on a business *is* binding on Aidan.

Why did equity decide to enforce negative covenants? The decision in *Tulk* v. *Moxhay* was based on the fact that the purchaser had notice of the covenant.

REVISION NOTE

The term 'notice' has a particular meaning in land law, and if you are still uncertain what it means, refer back to Chapter 1 now to revise this.

If the covenant is negative, the following other conditions must be satisfied before equity will enforce it against subsequent parties:

(a) *The covenantee must own land for the benefit of which the covenant was entered into.* See *LCC* v. *Allen* (1914).

(b) *The covenant must touch and concern the dominant land.* As mentioned above, the point here is the covenant must not be personal.

REVISION NOTE

Check Chapter 6 (leases) to revise what this term means.

(c) *It must be the common intention of the parties that the covenant shall run.* Covenants made on or after 1 January 1926 are deemed to be made with subsequent parties (s. 79, LPA 1925). Covenants made before that date will run if the language indicates this, e.g. 'the covenant is made by the covenantor for himself, his heirs and assigns'.

(d) *The covenantee must have notice of the covenant.*

   (i)   If title to the burdened land is registered, the covenant must be protected by a notice on the register of that title (s. 29, LRA 2002). If it is not, the covenant will not bind a purchaser.

   (ii) If title to the land is not registered and the covenant was entered into on or after 1 January 1926, it must be registered as a Class D(ii) land charge: otherwise it will not bind a purchaser.

   (iii) If title to the land is not registered and the covenant was entered into before 1 January 1926, the old notice rules apply and the covenant will not bind a purchaser unless he/she has notice of it (see Chapter 2 for a discussion of notice).

In effect, registration under (i) and (ii) above constitutes notice.

Note: if the covenant was not registered when Aidan bought Blackacre, it would not bind him. However, it could be registered after he bought it, and if Aidan sold Blackacre to Charles it would bind Charles.

REVISION NOTE

Check Chapter 2 for registered and unregistered land.

Covenant (c)

This is a covenant by the owner of Blackacre to contribute to the maintenance of the sewers which serve *both* Blackacre and Whiteacre. As such, it is a positive covenant and so it would not be enforceable against subsequent owners of Blackacre were it not for a special rule.

Covenants of this kind operate in situations where there are reciprocal benefits and burdens enjoyed by users of the facility. A mention of such a covenant in an examination question should lead you to mention this case:

KEY CASE

Halsall v. *Brizell* [1957] 1 All ER 371 (HC)

Concerning: positive covenants – an exception when they are binding on subsequent owners

Facts

Buyers of building plots covenanted that they would contribute to the cost of repairs of sewers and roads that were for the common use of the owners of all the building plots.

Legal principle

An agreement to contribute to the cost of these repairs was binding on a subsequent owner, on the principle that you cannot take the benefit of these rights yet avoid the burdens of them.

It is not clear when this principle applies. In *Rhone* v. *Stephens* (1994) Lord Templeman said that it would *not* apply when the owner had no choice whether to accept both the benefit and the burden. It is probably on this basis that mutual covenants between neighbours to maintain a fence between their respective properties would not come under *Halsall* v. *Brizell*.

 Make your answer stand out

Look at the judgment of Peter Gibson LJ in *Thamesmead Town Ltd* v. *Allotey* (1998) for a detailed consideration of when the *Halsall* v. *Brizell* principle can apply.

■ Situation four: enforcing the benefit at common law – the covenantee and successors in title

John sells Whiteacre to Eileen, Rosemary remains the owner of Blackacre. Can Eileen bring an action against Rosemary? This involves the question of whether the *benefit* of the covenant has passed to Eileen.

We have already seen in situation one that the covenantee (John) can enforce the standard covenants against the covenantor (Rosemary). We are now looking at whether successors in title to the covenantee can enforce the covenant, i.e. in our situation, whether Eileen can enforce the covenant. Remember that this will be enforcing the *benefit* of the covenant.

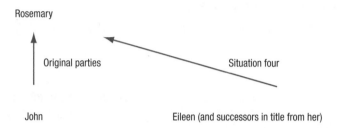

Rosemary

Original parties   Situation four

John   Eileen (and successors in title from her)

Note what was said in the introduction to situation three: common law and equity take different approaches and do not mix. The common law will allow Eileen, provided that certain conditions are met (see below) to enforce the covenants against Rosemary. This only applies to actions against *the original covenantor.*

Equitable rules will apply when we come to consider, in situation five, what happens when Rosemary sells Blackacre to Aidan.

The following conditions must be met for Eileen to able to show that the benefit of the covenant has passed to her and that she can sue Rosemary for breach of them:

(a) The covenant *must touch and concern the land* (*Rogers* v. *Hosegood* (1900)). See above under situation three for an explanation of this term.

(b) The original covenantee must have had a legal estate in the land which is benefited.

(c) The successor in title (Eileen) must have also acquired a legal estate in the land.

(d) The benefit of the covenant was intended by the original parties to run with the land.

Smith and Snipes Hall Farm v. *River Douglas Catchment Board* (1949) is a good illustration of this area.

Note: a covenant not to allow pets other than domestic pets on the land is often found and is considered to benefit the land (i.e. it touches and concerns the land).

■ Situation five: enforcing the benefit in equity – successors in title to both covenantee and covenantor

John sells Whiteacre to Eileen, Rosemary sells Blackacre to Aidan. Aidan is in breach of all the standard covenants. Can Eileen bring an action against Aidan? This involves whether the *benefit* has passed to Eileen and the burden has *passed* to Aidan.

Note that the above rules in situation four are of no help at all where Eileen wishes to sue Aidan. If Eileen is to have a right to enforce against Aidan, then this can only be in equity because, as we saw in situation three, Aidan is only liable in equity.

There are three methods under which Eileen can show that the benefit of a covenant has passed to her *in equity* by:

(a) annexation;
(b) assignment;
(c) proof of the existence of a building scheme.

Annexation

The benefit of the covenant is *attached to the land*, glued to it, in effect. Whoever acquires title to the land benefited by the covenant (the dominant land) also acquires the benefit of the covenant.

This can happen by:

- **Express annexation**. Look at the words of the deed which created the covenant. In an exam question you may be given the actual words in a conveyance and asked if they amount to an express annexation. Contrast the words used in *Rogers* v. *Hosegood* (1900) and *Renals* v. *Cowlishaw* (1878).

- **Implied annexation**. This is where there is no mention in the covenant that it benefits particular land and so any intention to annex the benefit of covenant to the land must be implied. See *Marten* v. *Flight Refuelling Ltd* (1962).

- **Statutory annexation**.

Section 78(1), LPA 1925

'A covenant relating to the land of the covenantee shall be deemed to be made with the covenantee and his successors in title.'

This includes all covenants which relate to the land but will not include personal covenants, e.g. 'to do X's shopping for her'.

The effect of *Federated Homes* v. *Mill Lodge Properties Ltd* (1980) is that the benefit of a covenant will be annexed to land even where there are no words of the kind in *Rogers* v. *Hosegood* and so the cases where the benefit will not be annexed will be few. This means that most cases will now fall under the heading of statutory annexation, although if the facts of an examination question are similar to those of *Rogers* v. *Hosegood* then it is as well to treat it as express annexation.

 Make your answer stand out

Federated Homes has not escaped criticism. Look at e.g. Newsome (1982).

! Don't be tempted to...

Make sure you check where the covenant cannot benefit the majority of the dominant land. See *Re Ballard's Conveyance* (1937) and *Earl of Leicester* v. *Wells-next-the-Sea UDC* (1972)).

Also, suppose that Whiteacre was divided by Eileen and she retained part and part was sold to Josephine. Could they both claim the benefit of the covenant? There is no clear answer here but it appears from *Federated Homes* that, unless the covenant clearly indicates that it is only to be annexed to the whole of the dominant land, the benefit will pass when the land is divided. Thus, it is likely that Josephine can enforce it.

Assignment

Its importance was diminished by *Federated Homes* which has made annexation the method of transferring the benefit of a covenant in the great majority of cases.

Roake v. *Chadha* (1983) is a good example.

By proof of the existence of a building scheme

This is often found in practice.

Example

John, instead of selling part of his land to Rosemary, decides to develop it all and to sell it in individual plots with houses on each plot. John wants the area to be kept tidy and to remain residential, as this will affect the price which he will be able to obtain for each plot. Therefore, he requires each buyer to enter the following covenants with both the developers and with all other owners:

(a) not to run a business from their house;
(b) not to erect any fences, walls, hedges, etc. in their front gardens.

The effect is to create a local law for that area and provided that the requirements for a building scheme are satisfied then these covenants are enforceable.

See *Elliston* v. *Reacher* (1908) for an example of the operation of a building scheme.

These requirements have been relaxed in more recent cases (see e.g. *Baxter* v. *Four Oaks Properties Ltd* (1965), but the essential feature remains: *there must have been a common intention that the purchaser would be subject to mutual restrictions which are reciprocal*, i.e. a local law.

Summary of situation five

The effect of combining the rule that a party can be bound in equity by a negative covenant (Aidan) with the rule that in equity a party can claim the benefit of a covenant (Eileen) is that Eileen can sue Aidan for breach of the covenant not to run a business on Blackacre.

■ Discharge of covenants

KEY STATUTE

Section 84(1), LPA 1925

The Lands Tribunal has power 'wholly or partly to discharge or modify' a restrictive covenant.

There are several grounds for this, for instance, that the covenant is obsolete, that it impedes reasonable use of the land, that the removal of the covenant would not injure those entitled to any benefit, or that they have agreed to the removal of the covenant. Compensation may be ordered to be paid to the person(s) entitled to the benefit of the covenant which was discharged or modified.

Remedies for breach of a restrictive covenant

- Injunction.
- Damages in lieu of an injunction.

> **EXAM TIP**
>
> Do not forget to mention remedies at the end of your answer. Students often do and lose marks.

Law Commission proposals for reform

In Consultation Paper 186, published in March 2008, the Law Commission provisionally proposed that:

- The existing rules on negative and positive covenants on freehold land should be replaced by a new land obligation which would be a legal interest in land and would include both positive and negative covenants. It would operate in broadly the same way as an easement with a requirement for both a dominant and servient tenement and the land obligation would have to be for the benefit of the dominant land. Land obligations could only be created expressly and where title is registered.

- Existing covenants would continue to operate so that there would be two regimes: land obligations and restrictive covenants. The Commission pointed out that a two-tier regime has applied to leasehold covenants since the coming into force of the Landlord and Tenant (Covenants) Act 1995.

- The Commission invited views on whether there should be any provision for automatic or triggered expiry of land obligations.

- The jurisdiction of the Lands Tribunal to discharge or modify a restrictive covenant under s. 84(1) of the LPA 1925 would also apply to land obligations and the grounds for the exercise of this jurisdiction would be made more transparent.

■Chapter summary: putting it all together

Test yourself

☐ Can you tick all the points from the **revision checklist** at the beginning of this chapter?

☐ Attempt the **sample question** from the beginning of this chapter using the answer guidelines below.

☐ Go to the **companion website** to access more revision support online, including interactive quizzes, sample questions with answer guidelines, 'You be the marker' exercises, flashcards and podcasts you can download.

Answer guidelines

See the problem question at the start of the chapter. A diagram illustrating how to structure your answer is available on the companion website.

Approaching the question

Do not be afraid of problem questions on this area. A calm, logical approach will get you good marks.

Important points to include

1 Action by Eileen against Aidan. Eileen must prove that:

 ■ her land has the benefit of the covenants;

 ■ Aidan's land has the burden of the covenants.

2 Consider Aidan first:

 ■ **Covenant (a)**: negative (*Tulk* v. *Moxhay*) so burden may pass – go through conditions for this to happen (*LCC* v. *Allen* etc.) and note also that the covenants must be registered. The question says that title to the land is registered and so answer for only registered land. If the question does not say whether it is registered then answer for both registered and unregistered land.

- **Covenant (b)**: positive (*Austerberry* v. *Oldham Corporation*), so Aidan cannot be bound, although Rosemary remains liable on the covenant.
- **Covenant (c)**: *Halsall* v. *Brizell* situation.

3 Now consider Eileen.

- Eileen can sue Aidan under (a) if the benefit has passed to her in equity. The covenants are expressed to be made for the benefit of Whiteacre so this may be enough (see *Rogers* v. *Hosegood*) but in any case on the basis of *Federated Homes* (applying s. 78(1) of the LPA 1925) there is probably statutory annexation.
- Aidan not liable under (b)
- Eileen can sue Aidan under (c) under the benefit–burden principle.

Finally, do not forget remedies: injunction plus damages?

 Make your answer stand out

Look at each of these points:

- Uncertainty if *Halsall* v. *Brizell* applies, note case law.
- Mention Law Commission proposals for reform.

READ TO IMPRESS

Law Commission Report 127, 'Transfer of land: The law of positive and restrictive covenants' (1984).

Law Commission Consultation Paper 186, Easements, covenants and profits à prendre (2008).

Newsome, 'Universal annexation' (1982) 98 LQR 202.

NOTES

NOTES

NOTES

Easements and profits

8

Revision checklist

Essential points you should know:

- [ ] What is an easement and what is a profit
- [ ] Characteristics of easements and profits
- [ ] When an easement and a profit is a legal interest and when an equitable interest
- [ ] How easements and profits can be created
- [ ] How rules on profits differ from easements
- [ ] Law Commission proposals for reform

Topic map

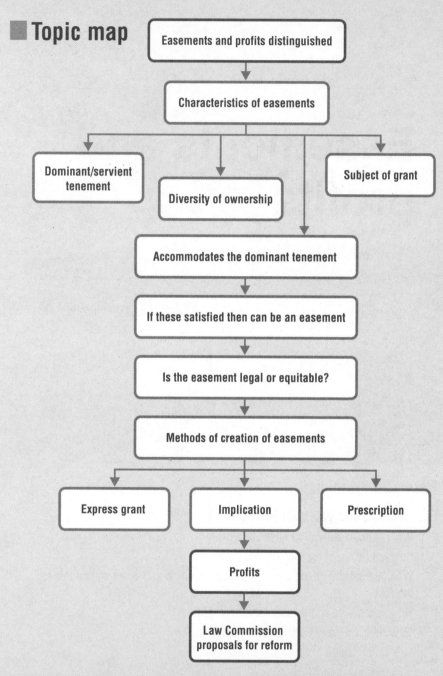

Easements and profits distinguished

↓

Characteristics of easements

↓

Dominant/servient tenement

Diversity of ownership

Subject of grant

↓

Accommodates the dominant tenement

↓

If these satisfied then can be an easement

↓

Is the easement legal or equitable?

↓

Methods of creation of easements

↓

Express grant

Implication

Prescription

↓

Profits

↓

Law Commission proposals for reform

A printable version of this topic map is available from **www.pearsoned.co.uk/lawexpress**

■Introduction

Questions are usually on easements but watch for one on a profit, e.g. on grazing rights. Watch for a possible connection with licences (Chapter 5) and with land registration – check Chapter 2. The basic principles are fairly straightforward but do watch for tricky areas such as the application of the rule in *Wheeldon* v. *Burrows* and the grant of easements under s. 62 of the LPA 1925. In addition, in any answer you will gain extra marks by mentioning the proposals for reform contained in the Law Commission Consultation Paper 186, which are referred to in this chapter and summarised at the end.

ASSESSMENT ADVICE

Essay questions This is a good subject for essays. Topics include:

■ Can new negative easements be created?

■ Rules on the grant of implied easements.

■ Possible reform of the law on acquisition of easements by prescription. This is now very topical in view of the Law Commission Consultation Paper – see below.

Problem questions Problem questions usually follow a familiar pattern which requires you to deal with the following areas. You must address all of these issues

■ Can the right be an easement or a profit at all? At this stage you may eliminate some of the rights which may be only licences.

■ If it is, is it legal or equitable? This will involve you in considering the third point:

■ Was it correctly created?

■Sample question

Could you answer this question? Below is a typical essay question that could arise on this topic. Guidelines on answering the question are included at the end of the chapter, while a sample problem question and guidance on tackling it can be found on the companion website.

Many easements are implied rather than created by express grant. Critically analyse the methods by which easements can be created by implication.

Easements and profits distinguished

Similarities: both easements and profits (in full, profits à prendre) are proprietary interests in land.

Differences: easements are rights over the land of another, e.g. rights to light, rights of way.

Profits are rights to enter on the land of another and take the profits of it.

This chapter now deals mainly with easements and looks at profits at the end. This is because you are more likely to get exam questions on easements.

Characteristics of easements

These are from *Re Ellenborough Park* (1955):

A dominant and a servient tenement

The easement must benefit land and there must be two pieces of land:

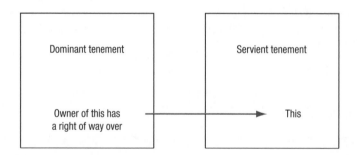

Diversity of ownership

The dominant tenement (DT) and the servient tenement (ST) must be owned or occupied by different persons.

Accommodates the dominant tenement

This really means that the easement must benefit the land (DT) as such and not the present owner nor activities which the present owner is carrying on.

Hill v. *Tupper* (1863) 2 H & C 121 (HC)

Concerning: easement must accommodate (benefit) the DT

Facts

The owner of a canal granted X the exclusive right to put pleasure boats on the canal for profit.

Legal principle

Such a right is just a personal right which did not benefit the land as such.

The question is whether a business carried on on the land is so closely connected with the land that it does benefit it. This seems to be the explanation of *Moody* v. *Steggles* (1879). You may need to contrast these cases in an exam.

The DT and the ST must be reasonably adjacent otherwise there could be no benefit.

Example

X claims a right of way over land owned by Y but Y's land is two miles away. Although it may benefit X to have the right of way, it can hardly be said to benefit X's land.

Subject of grant

The right claimed must be capable of forming the subject matter of a grant. The basic point is that the right must be sufficiently certain.

X claims that Y should not build on his land as it would spoil X's view.

A right to a view is not certain enough to be an easement (*Aldred's Case* (1610)).

X should have obtained a restrictive covenant over Y's land. Check Chapter 7.

Easements should not involve the owner of the ST in positive obligations

See *Regis Property* v. *Redman* (1956).

 Make your answer stand out

There are cases where positive easements have been allowed – e.g. easement of fencing. (See *Crow* v. *Wood* (1971).)

No new negative easements?

KEY CASE

Phipps v. *Pears* [1964] 2 All ER 35 (HC)

Concerning: the creation of new negative easements (i.e. owner of ST has no actual obligations but is restricted in the use of the land)

Facts

Claim to an easement to protection of one house from rain and frost by another house. This would mean that the other house could not be demolished. The claim was rejected.

Legal principle

The courts are reluctant to allow the creation of new negative easements which would be an undue restriction on an owner's rights over his land.

 Make your answer stand out

This case was distinguished in *Rees* v. *Skerrett* (2001). Mention this case in an essay question.

An easement cannot subsequently be used for a different purpose

This covers intensification of use (*Jelbert* v. *Davis* (1968)).

Easement cannot amount to exclusive use: ouster principle.

A distinction must be drawn between an easement and a lease or a licence.

KEY CASE

Copeland v. *Greenhalf* [1952] 1 All ER 809 (HC)

Concerning: claim to an easement where there is exclusive use

Facts

The claimant owned land on which the defendant had stored and repaired vehicles for 50 years. He claimed an easement by prescription.

Legal principle

This was a claim to beneficial use of the land and so could not be an easement. Upjohn J described it as: 'virtually a claim to possession of the servient tenement.'

 Make your answer stand out

The ouster principle has not been consistently applied: see e.g. *Wright* v. *McAdam* (1949) – below.

Car parking

This is a likely area for an exam question because:

- Whether there can be an easement of the right to park a car has not been definitively settled although there have been many cases – see e.g. *Batchelor* v. *Marlow* (2001). Note that *Moncrieff* v. *Jamieson* (2007) dealt with Scottish law.

- If there is an easement then how does the ouster principle (above) affect it? Suppose that X claims the right to park her car on a defined space on land owned by Y. In *Moncrieff* v. *Jamieson* Lord Scott in the HL proposed the test of whether the servient owner 'retains possession and, subject to the reasonable exercise of the right in question, control of the servient land'. The Law Commission, in its Consultation Paper, thought that it was difficult to define control and preferred to ask: 'What can the dominant owner do?' Thus any right must be clearly defined (see paras. 3.34–3.55).

- See Hill-Smith (2007) and also the excellent example at para. 3.52 of the Law Commission Consultation Paper.

> ✓ Make your answer stand out
>
> In a general question on the creation or nature of easements mention also:
>
> Creation of easements by statute, examples:
>
> ■ Access to Neighbouring Land Act 1992;
> ■ Party Wall Act 1996.

■ Easements, profits and third parties

REVISION NOTE

> The rules were set out in Chapter 2 and you should refer to this now to check your knowledge.

Summary

Registered land

- Legal easements and profits created expressly (i.e. by deed) are registrable dispositions.
- Express legal easements and profits, and equitable easements, which were overriding before 13 October 2003, remain overriding.
- New equitable easements and profits are now minor interests.
- The only new legal easements and profits that can be overriding are those created:
  - by implied reservation
  - by implied grant (rule in *Wheeldon* v. *Burrows* or s. 62(1), LPA 1925)
  - by prescription (Sch. 3, para. 3, LRA 2002).

Unregistered land

- Legal easements are binding on all third parties.
- Equitable easements must be registered as land charges if created on or after 1 January 1926. Those created before this date will bind purchasers who have notice of them and will bind donees automatically.

Creation of easements

Expressly

- Legal – deed.
- Equitable – written agreement.

REVISION NOTE

You should check Chapter 1 and revise the rules on the creation of legal interests in land by deed and equitable interests by written agreement.

Implied reservation in a conveyance

- Necessity e.g. access to land-locked land. A good recent case is *Adealon International Corp. Proprietary Ltd* v. *Merton LBC* (2007).
- Common intention. See *Wong* v. *Beaumont Property Trust Ltd* (1965).

Estoppel

REVISION NOTE

Check Chapter 5 for estoppel. A good case on estoppel easements for the exam is *Ives Investments Ltd* v. *High* (1967).

Acquisition of implied easements under the rule in *Wheeldon* v. *Burrows*

KEY CASE

***Wheeldon* v. *Burrows* (1879) 12 Ch D 31 (HC)**
Concerning: acquisition of an easement by implied grant

To summarise the facts of this case would add little to an understanding of the legal principle outlined below. Remember that examiners are looking for an understanding of the ratio and legal principle, and that only reciting the facts in an exam will not improve your grade.

Legal principle
On a grant of land, the grantee (e.g. the buyer) will acquire, by implication, all easements which:

- are continuous and apparent;
- have been and are at the time of the grant used by the grantor for the benefit of the land.

> **!** **Don't be tempted to...**
>
> Make sure that you are clear about when a situation can involve *Wheeldon* v. *Burrows*. A useful guide is to look for a plot of land which is originally in the ownership of one person and is then subdivided.

EXAM TIP

> *Wheeldon* v. *Burrows* easements operate in favour of the buyer and against the seller.

This is how a *Wheeldon* v. *Burrows* situation works:

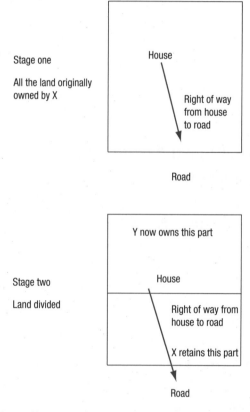

Stage one

All the land originally owned by X

House

Right of way from house to road

Road

Stage two

Land divided

Y now owns this part

House

Right of way from house to road

X retains this part

Road

The rule in *Wheeldon* v. *Burrows* allows Y to claim as an implied easement a right of way over the land retained by X.

The rule in *Wheeldon* v. *Burrows* also applies where X in the above example sells all the land and grants part of the land to one person (Y) in our example, and grants the other part to Z (i.e. the part retained by X in our example). Therefore, X no longer retains any land.

Are easements created by the rule in *Wheeldon* v. *Burrows* legal or equitable?

This depends on the document which transferred the land (e.g. the document under which X transferred to Y).

If it was a deed (which it would be here), the easement will be legal, but if was simply by an enforceable written agreement, it will be equitable.

REVISION NOTE

Go back to Chapter 1 and check that you understand the distinction between deeds and written agreements.

Acquisition of implied easements under s. 62(1) of the LPA 1925

KEY STATUTE

Section 62(1), LPA 1925

A conveyance of the land shall be deemed to convey and shall operate to convey with the land all privileges, easements, rights appertaining or reputed to appertain to the land at the time of conveyance.

This provision is not controversial in itself: it merely provides that on a conveyance of land certain rights that it has (e.g. easements and profits) are automatically also conveyed. What is controversial is the use which has been made of it to create easements where none seemed to exist before.

Wright v. *McAdam* [1949] 2 All ER 556 (CA)

Concerning: the operation of s. 62(1), LPA 1925 so that it creates new easements in addition to transferring existing easements

Facts

The defendant let a flat to the claimant and gave her permission (i.e. a licence) to store coal in it. He later granted her a new tenancy.

Legal principle

The grant of the tenancy was a conveyance under s. 62(1), and as a right to store coal was a right capable of being granted by law the grant of the new tenancy had the effect of converting what was a licence into an easement.

Permission to store coal (Licence)   New lease   Permission now an easement

EXAM TIP

Check that the right is capable of being an easement. In fact in *Wright* v. *McAdam* the right of storage appeared to be exclusive, which might not have qualified it for an easement. (See discussion of the ouster principle above.)

Another example is *International Tea Stores Co.* v. *Hobbs* (1903).

In *Sovmots Investments Ltd* v. *Environment Secretary* (1977) it was considered that diversity of occupation is needed for s. 62 to apply, i.e. it is necessary for each piece of land to be occupied by different people. This has now been doubted in *P & S Platt Ltd* v. *Crouch* (2003), i.e. s. 62 can apply where land is owned by the same person.

! Don't be tempted to...

Do not apply the decision in *Platt* uncritically. It is open to the serious objection that rights cannot be apparent if they are exercised by an owner over his/her own land as there is no need for a right as such to be able to do this. So still use *Wheeldon* v. *Burrows* where the land was originally occupied by the same person but mention this case too. See the answer guidelines at the end of this chapter for an illustration.

Prescription

This is not likely to be the subject of a whole exam question but it can form part of it.

KEY DEFINITION: Prescription

Acquisition of easements and profits by long use.

Conditions for prescription

Use must be without:

- force;
- secrecy;
- permission.

Types of prescription

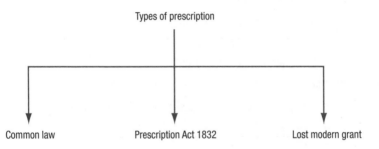

Types of prescription

Common law   Prescription Act 1832   Lost modern grant

- *Common law* – from 'time immemorial' – 1189 – in practice for as long as anyone can remember and it could have been since 1189.

EXAM TIP

If the DT is a house, then this method cannot apply as the house will not have existed in 1189.

- Under the Prescription Act 1832.

KEY STATUTE

Section 2, Prescription Act 1832

Claim to an easement by prescription requires 20 years' continuous use, but where the easement was exercised with the oral agreement of the servient owner, it is 40 years.

A claim by prescription is based on a presumed grant and the claim will fail if the presumed grantor had no capacity to grant the easement. (See *Housden* v. *Conservators of Wimbledon and Putney Common* (2008).) See Bridge (2009).)

Note the periods for profits: 30 and 60 years.

Section 3, Prescription Act 1832

Claim to an easement of light requires 20 years' continuous use – no provision for an extra 20 years where exercised with the permission of the owner.

Note: Rights of Light Act 1959: owner of ST can block a right to light by registering a notice.

Section 4, Prescription Act 1832

The periods must be 'next before' the action.

See example below under 'lost modern grant'.

- Discontinuance for less than a year is ignored.

The relationship between these sections is shown by this example:

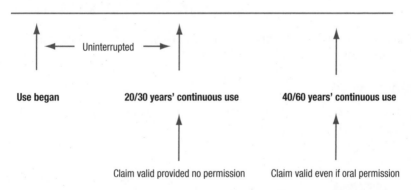

- *Lost modern grant.* In an exam question this should be mentioned as the last possibility.

The court assumes two things that have not, in fact, occurred:

- there was a grant of an easement;
- it has been lost.

Example

This is based on a profit.

X has allowed his sheep to graze on Y's land for many years but did not do so for the last 18 months because they were diseased.

- No claim to a profit at common law: cannot prove use since 1189.
- Prescription Act does not apply as discontinuance more than a year – s. 4 applies – no period of prescription as period not next before action.
- So, have to rely on lost modern grant.

See *Tehidy Minerals* v. *Norman* (1971) for a case example.

■ Profits

Check carefully what the right is: an easement or a profit.

Note the following rules on profits and how they differ from those on easements:

- No requirement of a dominant tenement.
- The rule in *Wheeldon* v. *Burrows* does not apply to the creation of profits but s. 62(1), LPA 1925 does.
- The periods of prescription are longer: see above.
- Apart from this, the rules are generally the same.

■ Law Commission proposals for reform

In Consultation Paper 186, published in March 2008, the Law Commission provisionally proposed that:

- Any right must be clearly defined, or be capable of clear definition, and not involve the unrestricted use of the servient land (para. 3.55).

- Easements should no longer be capable of creation by implication under s. 62(1) of the LPA 1925. In addition it asked whether the law on acquisition of easements by implication should be recast into statutory form (paras. 4.104, 4.149).

- The present rules law on acquisition of easements by prescription should be abolished and replaced by a one single method of acquisition by prescription with a proposed period of 20 years (para. 4.221). The paper also asked if acquisition by prescription should be possible at all and if it could be replaced by proprietary estoppel, which the Commission does not favour (para. 4.193).

- Profits should only be acquired by express grant, reservation or statute and not by prescription (para. 16.31).

- Easements created by implication and easements in unregistered land should be capable of extinguishment after non-use after a set period of time. This would not apply to express easements in registered land (para. 5.63).

- Section 84(1) of the LPA 1925 (see Chapter 7) should also allow the discharge or modification of easements or profits (para. 14.41).

■ Chapter summary: putting it all together

Test yourself

- ☐ Can you tick all the points from the **revision checklist** at the beginning of this chapter?
- ☐ Attempt the **sample question** from the beginning of this chapter using the answer guidelines below.
- ☐ Go to the **companion website** to access more revision support online, including interactive quizzes, sample questions with answer guidelines, 'You be the marker' exercises, flashcards and podcasts you can download.

Answer guidelines

See the essay question at the start of the chapter.

Approaching the question

This question asks for not only an explanation of the methods by which easements are acquired by implication but also a critical analysis. Keep this in mind!

Important points to include

Explain what acquisition by implication means and how it contrasts with express acquisition.

Move on to the main methods of acquisition by implication – see above – and make sure that, in particular, you explain creation by *Wheeldon* v. *Burrows* and s. 62(1) of the LPA 1925 clearly.

Emphasise recent cases in this area and demonstrate a clear knowledge of how the decision in the *Platt* case *may* have expanded the scope of s. 62 acquisition of easements at the expense of *Wheeldon* v. *Burrows*.

A possible conclusion would be that the present law is complex and confusing and to ask whether there is any need for implied creation of easements.

You should then end by looking at the ideas in the Law Commission Consultation Paper – see summary above

 Make your answer stand out

Consider the practical problems for a purchaser created by implied easements and look at the report of *Moncrieff* v. *Jamieson,* which was also a case of implied creation of an easement (of parking) attached to an express grant of a right of way. Discuss the potential problems to which this decision gives rise as explained in the article by Junior (see further reading, below.)

You could also question whether s. 62(1) does create new easements by implication or expressly, i.e. by the express word of the statute.

READ TO IMPRESS

Bridge, 'Prescriptive easements: capacity to grant' (2009) 68(1) CLJ 40.

Hill-Smith, 'Rights of parking and the ouster principle after *Batchelor* v. *Marlow*' [2007] Conv 223.

Junior, 'Warning – Parking problems ahead (*Moncrieff* v. *Jamieson* applied)' (2008) 1 SLT 1.

Lawson, 'Easements', in Tee (ed.), *Land Law, Issues, Debates, Policy*, Willan, Uffculme (2002).

Law Commission Consultation Paper 186, 'Easements, covenants and profits à prendre' (2008).

NOTES

Mortgages

9

■ Topic map

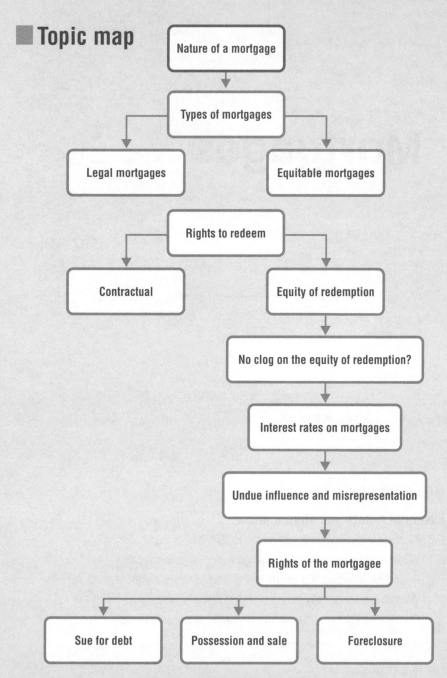

A printable version of this topic map is available from **www.pearsoned.co.uk/lawexpress**

■ Introduction

This topic is not difficult and is more heavily weighted to case law than the others. It also involves the intervention of equity and, although you do not need a detailed knowledge of equity to answer these questions, it will help if you stress the importance of equitable principles such as the need to strike down unconscionable bargains.

ASSESSMENT ADVICE

Essay question Essays may deal with:

- General principles on which the courts can intervene to strike down clauses in mortgage deeds;
- The remedies available to the mortgagee;
- Undue influence.

Problem question Problem questions usually involve a number of clauses in a mortgage which you need to examine to see if they are liable to be struck down on the grounds that they are oppressive, unconscionable, etc. A sound knowledge of the cases is needed but this is an area on which you should aim to score highly.

The problem may also involve undue influence although this can arise in an equity exam.

■ Sample question

Could you answer this question? Below is a typical essay question that could arise on this topic. Guidelines on answering the question are included at the end of the chapter, while a sample problem question and guidance on tackling it are included on the companion website.

ESSAY QUESTION

'If the freedom of home-owners to make economic use of their homes is not to be frustrated, a bank must be able to have confidence that a wife's signature of the necessary guarantee and charge will be binding on her.' Lord Nicholls in *Royal Bank of Scotland plc (No. 2)* v. *Etridge* (2001).

To what extent do you consider that the present law on this area does enable banks to have this necessary confidence?

Nature of a mortgage

KEY DEFINITION: Mortgagee and mortgagor

The lender is the **mortgagee**, and the borrower is the **mortgagor**.

The simple idea of a mortgage is that it is security for loan. In fact, a mortgage is both:

- A contract between the mortgagor and the mortgagee;
- A proprietary interest in the land of the mortgagor granted to the mortgagee.

If a mortgage was only a contract, then this would not give the mortgagee enough security as if the land was sold then the mortgagor would not have to repay the mortgage before he/she sold the land. Therefore, it must also give an interest in the land.

Types of mortgages

A mortgage of land is normally a charge by deed by way of legal mortgage.

This will be legal but an equitable mortgage can be created by an agreement which complies with s. 2 of the Law of Property (Miscellaneous Provisions) Act 1989.

REVISION NOTE

Check in Chapter 1 that you can recall these provisions.

Rights to redeem

Redemption of the mortgage means simply paying it off so that the land is free from the mortgage.

| Date of mortgage | Contractual date: usually six months later | Equity of redemption now takes over |

Make your answer stand out

Equity played a major part in developing the law on mortgages and this is for historical reasons.

Mortgages were traditionally entered into when someone needed a loan as they were in debt and so they might be persuaded into a mortgage on terms which were very onerous and so equity aimed to protect them. Today mortgages are usually made because a person wishes to buy or lease a house. However, equity still insists on the equity of redemption, and it claims the right to set a mortgage aside (see below). Read Oldham (2002).

! Don't be tempted to...

Be sure that you understand exactly when the courts can intervene to set aside the terms of a mortgage. This can arise:

- In an essay;
- In a problem question, where you can gain extra marks by not just quoting cases which deal with the particular point but also stressing that in the background there is a debate on the precise extent to which the courts can intervene.

Note Greene MR in the *Knightsbridge* case (1939) (below): 'But equity does not reform commercial transactions because they are unreasonable. It is concerned to see two things – one that the essential requirements of a mortgage transaction are observed, and the other that oppressive or unconscionable terms are not enforced.'

Note the distinction drawn by Greene MR between 'unreasonable' and 'oppressive or unconscionable'.

 Make your answer stand out

Read Houghton and Livesey (2001). This gives an excellent survey of the law in the light of current social trends.

■ Equity of redemption

A fundamental principle is that the mortgagor must be able to redeem early. However, as this is equity this is not an absolute rule:

KEY CASE

Knightsbridge Estates Trust Ltd v. *Byrne* [1939] Ch 441 (HC)

Concerning: early redemption of a mortgage

Facts

A commercial mortage at ordinary interest rates where there was no inequality of bargaining power provided that it could not be redeemed for 40 years. The borrower was not allowed to repay earlier.

Legal principle

There is no absolute rule that a mortgage cannot prevent early redemption.

KEY CASE

Fairclough v. *Swan Brewery* [1912] AC 565 (PC)

Concerning: when postponement of the right to redeem a mortgage is void

Facts

The mortgagor was an assignee of a lease which had seventeen and a half years to run. The final mortgage instalment was due only six weeks before the lease expired.

Legal principle

Where the redemption date of the mortgage on a lease is at the point when the lease is about to expire, then redemption is of no value to the mortgagor. Therefore, the mortgagor was entitled to redeem earlier.

No clog on the equity of redemption?

This means that on redemption all mortgage obligations must be discharged but, in fact, the courts have not always applied this rule rigidly.

KEY CASE

Krelinger v. New Patagonia Meat and Cold Storage Co. Ltd **[1914] AC 25 (HL)**

Concerning: whether a collateral advantage in a mortgage can continue after it has been redeemed

Facts

A firm of woolbrokers lent money on a mortgage which could be repaid at any time in the next five years. The mortgagor also agreed to give the mortgagee first refusal on all their sheepskins and to pay commission on any sold to a third party. This agreement was to last for the full five years. This collateral agreement was upheld.

Legal principle

A collateral advantage for the mortgagee may be upheld where it does not prevent the mortgagor getting his land back in the same form as when it was mortgaged.

Equity also regards a term of the mortgage that gives the mortgagee an option to purchase as a clog on the equity of redemption. See *Samuel* v. *Jarrah Timber* (1904).

 Make your answer stand out

The House of Lords came to this conclusion in *Samuel* v. *Jarrah Timber* with reluctance and it may reconsider this rule in future. Compare *Reeve* v. *Lisle* (1902) where the term was in a separate agreement and was upheld. In *Warnborough* v. *Garmite Ltd* (2003) it was held that the rule in *Samuel* v. *Jarrah* would not apply where the mortgage was part of a more complex transaction. Here the mortgage was part of a sale and purchase agreement.

Another instance of a clog on the equity of redemption is provided by *Noakes* v. *Rice* (1902).

Interest rates on mortgages

These are subject to the general principle that equity will set aside a bargain which is oppressive and unconscionable.

Look at *Cityland and Property (Holdings) Ltd* v. *Dabrah* (1968) and *Multiservice Bookbinding* v. *Marden* (1978) and note the different approaches in each.

KEY STATUTE

Sections 140A and 140B, Consumer Credit Act 1974 (inserted by ss. 19 and 20, Consumer Credit Act 2006)

The courts have wide powers over a credit agreement (including a mortgage agreement) where it is unfair to the debtor (i.e. the mortgagor) because of any of its terms, the way in which it is exercised, or any other thing done by the creditor (i.e. the mortgagee).

EXAM TIP

Check if the lender is an individual or a company. If the latter, then this Act will not apply.

EXAM TIP

The new s. 140 replaces the previous ss. 137–140 of the Consumer Credit Act 1974.

■ Undue influence and mortgages

Undue influence is an equitable doctrine that is difficult to define precisely but, in essence, it aims to prevent the vulnerable from exploitation. It is really directed at the manner in which a transaction is entered into.

You should check if it is likely to be examined in land law, as it can also arise in an equity exam, but it is certainly relevant to mortgages.

KEY CASE

Royal Bank of Scotland plc v. *Etridge (No. 2)* **[2001] 4 All ER 449 (HL)**
Concerning: what undue influence is

Facts

The facts of this case would add little to an understanding of the legal principle which follows. Remember that examiners are usually looking for an understanding of the ratio and legal principle and that reciting the facts in an exam will not improve your grade.

Legal principle

Lord Nicholls held that there is a distinction between:

(a) cases of actual coercion;
(b) cases where the undue influence arises from a particular relationship.

In (b) there is a subdivision between:

(i) Cases where there is a relationship of trust and confidence. If it is established that there has been a transaction which calls for some explanation, then the burden shifts to the person seeking to uphold the transaction to show that there was no undue influence.

(ii) Certain types of relationship where one party has acquired influence over another who is vulnerable and dependent and by whom substantial gifts are not normally to be expected, e.g. parent and child, trustee and beneficiary and medical adviser and patient. In these cases there is a presumption of undue influence by the stronger party over the weaker.

EXAM TIP

The most likely area of undue influence for an exam question is (b) (ii) above. It should be noted that (b) (ii) does not include husband and wife, a common scenario for exam problems and so this situation would fall into (b) (i).

! Don't be tempted to...

Remember to deal with the presumption of undue influence in a question on mortgages. Having first decided that you are dealing with a possible undue influence case, you should move on immediately to see where in the above categories it falls. This is vital to know if undue influence has to be proved or not.

Undue influence can affect a mortgage in two ways:

1 Where the mortgagee has exercised undue influence to induce the mortgagor to enter into the mortgage. A possible example is *National Westminster Bank* v. *Morgan* (1985).

2 Where the mortgagee has not exercised undue influence but it is claimed that a third party has and this affects the mortgagee. This is the most likely scenario for the exam.

Undue influence and third parties

This area has become of great importance in recent years especially since the decision of the House of Lords in *Barclays Bank* v. *O'Brien* (1994).

Students often jump straight to this issue when they see it in a problem question and do not first ask if there has been undue influence in the first place. Do this first!

Example

John persuades Claud, his partner, to enter into a second mortgage of their jointly owned home to the Viper Bank in order to secure some business debts of John. It is clear that John exercised undue influence over Claud to persuade him to sign. The question is whether the Viper Bank is affected by what John has done. If it is not, then, although John may be liable to Claud, the actual mortgage is unaffected.

EXAM TIP

The principles stated by Lord Browne-Wilkinson in *Barclays Bank* v. *O'Brien* were the starting point of the law here. However, they have been overtaken by those stated by Lord Nicholls in *Etridge* (below), and in a problem question you should concentrate on applying these.

Note: in the case below the word 'surety' is used and here it means the person who has agreed to guarantee the debt etc. – Claud in the above example.

KEY CASE

***Royal Bank of Scotland plc (No. 2)* v. *Etridge* [2001] 4 All ER 449 (HL)**

Concerning: (a) when a lender is put on inquiry, and (b) steps which a lender should take to avoid being affected by the undue influence of another, e.g. the borrower

Facts

The facts of this case would add little to an understanding of the legal principle which follows. Remember that examiners are usually looking for an understanding of the ratio and legal principle and that reciting the facts in an exam will not improve your grade.

Legal principles

These were stated by Lord Nicholls as follows:

(a) A lender is put on inquiry when one person offers to stand surety for the debts of:

- His or her spouse;
- A person involved in a non-commercial relationship with the surety and the lender is aware of this;
- Any company in which any of the above hold shares.

(b) Steps to be taken when a lender is put on enquiry:

- The lender must contact the surety and request that they nominate a solicitor.
- The surety must reply nominating a solicitor.
- The lender must, with the consent of the surety, disclose to the solicitor all relevant information – both the debtor's financial position and the details of the proposed loan.
- The solicitor must advise the surety in a face-to-face meeting at which the debtor is not present. The advice must cover an explanation of the documentation, the risks to the surety in signing and emphasise that the surety must decide whether to proceed.
- The solicitor must, if satisfied that the surety wishes to proceed, send written confirmation to the lender that the solicitor has explained the nature of the documents and their implications for the surety.

✓ Make your answer stand out

The principle in *O'Brien* and the decision in *Etridge* (above) have been the subject of a great deal of academic debate. A good place to start is the article by Andrews (2002).

Consequences of undue influence

If the mortgage is affected by undue influence, then it is voidable.

❗ Don't be tempted to...

Make sure that you deal with the *extent* to which the mortgage will be set aside. *TSB Bank plc* v. *Camfield* (1995): the whole mortgage was set aside. *Dunbar Bank plc* v. *Nadeem* (1997): it was only set aside on condition that the claimant accounted to the mortgagee for the benefit which she had from it.

Misrepresentation and mortgages

Instead of or in addition to the possibility of undue influence, an exam question may ask you if there has been misrepresentation. You will probably not need to remember much on this from your contract days, just the definition:

KEY DEFINITION: Misrepresentation

An untrue statement of fact which induces a person to enter into a transaction.

Look out for where undue influence and misrepresentation are possibly combined, i.e. X uses undue influence to persuade Y his partner, to sign a mortgage but also lies about how much the mortgage is for.

✓ Make your answer stand out

Read Thompson (2003), 'Mortgages and Undue Influence'. It provides an excellent critical study of the law.

 # Rights of the mortgagee

To sue for debt

■ A contractual right and allows the mortgagee to recover the debt.

Possession and sale

Possession

■ Allows the mortgagee to take possession (the mortgage deed allows this at any time during the mortgage) and to sell the property. Any surplus belongs to the mortgagor.

Where the mortgagee cannot obtain vacant possession from the mortgagor by negotiation and it is still occupied, then the mortgagee must seek possession by a court order.

KEY STATUTE

Section 36, Administration of Justice Act 1970

This applies to mortgages of dwelling houses and allows the court, if it appears that the mortgagor will, within a reasonable period, be able to pay sums due under the mortgage, or remedy a default consisting of a breach arising under it, to:

- Adjourn the proceedings; or

- On giving an order for possession, to stay or suspend execution of it or postpone the date for delivery of possession.

See *Cheltenham & Gloucester BS* v. *Norgan* (1996) for the principles on which this should be exercised.

Sale

An exam question may ask you if a mortgagee can apply to sell the mortgaged property. There are two key statutory provisions:

KEY STATUTE

Section 101(1) and (4), LPA 1925

Section 101(1): the mortgagee's statutory power of sale arises when:

- The mortgage was by deed;

- The mortgage money has become due (i.e. the redemption date has passed) or an instalment of the mortgage repayments are due.

Section 101(4) provides that for the above conditions to apply the mortgage must contain no expression of a contrary intention.

If the conditions in s. 101 are met, you then need to ask if the power of sale is actually exercisable.

Section 103, LPA 1925

A power of sale is exercisable if any one of these conditions are met:

- A notice requiring payment of the mortgage money due has been served and the mortgagor has been in default for three months following this.
- Interest under the mortgage has remained unpaid for two months after becoming due.
- There has been a breach of some mortgage term other than one for the payment of money or interest.

When selling, the mortgagee can have regard to his own interests and does not sell as trustee for the mortgagor (*Cuckmere Brick Co. Ltd* v. *Mutual Finance* (1971)). Thus, the mortgagee can have regard to his interests before those of the mortgagor.

Any surplus on the sale after all liabilities, costs and expenses have been met belongs to the mortgagor but, as the mortgagee, when selling, does not have to consider the mortgagor's interests, any surplus may be small as the mortgagee may not sell for the best price.

Foreclosure

- Rarely granted – vests the property in the mortgagee and the mortgagor has no rights to any surplus.

A reference to the ECHR and its application to actions for possession of land will earn you extra marks in an answer on the remedies of the mortgagee. Look at the discussion in Chapter 1.

■Chapter summary: putting it all together

Test yourself

- ☐ Can you tick all the points from the **revision checklist** at the beginning of this chapter?
- ☐ Attempt the **sample question** from the beginning of this chapter using the answer guidelines below.
- ☐ Go to the **companion website** to access more revision support online, including interactive quizzes, sample questions with answer guidelines, 'You be the marker' exercises, flashcards and podcasts you can download.

Answer guidelines

See essay question at the start of the chapter.

Approaching the question

This question does not require a general description of the law on third parties and undue influence but a carefully structured discussion of the actual issue. The background: the example given on page 176 of third parties and undue influence would make a good start.

Important points to include

- ■ Explain what undue influence and misrepresentation is.
- ■ Mention *Barclays Bank* v. *O'Brien* and how it began the development of this part of the law.
- ■ Explain *Etridge* and discuss whether the balance between the interests of banks, lenders and sureties is maintained by the principles in *Etridge*.

 Make your answer stand out

Reference to Lord Nicholls's speech in *Etridge* and to the views of academic authors – see further reading, below, and especially Thompson.

READ TO IMPRESS

Andrews, 'Undue influence – where's the disadvantage?' [2002] Conv 456.

Houghton and Livesey, 'Mortgage conditions: old law for a new century?', in Cooke (ed.), *Modern Studies in Property Law*, Vol. 1, Hart Publishing, Oxford (2001).

Oldham, 'Mortgages', in Tee (ed.), *Land Law, Issues, Debates, Policy*, Willan, Uffculme (2002).

Thompson 'Mortgages and undue influence', in Cooke (ed.), *Modern Studies in Property Law*, Vol. 2, Hart Publishing, Oxford (2003).

NOTES

10

Adverse possession

Revision checklist

Essential points you should know:

- [ ] Meaning of factual possession and intention to possess
- [ ] Relevance of an acknowledgement of the owner's title
- [ ] Significance of the land being earmarked
- [ ] Mechanics of acquiring title: unregistered land and registered land
- [ ] Impact of the Human Rights Act

■ Topic map

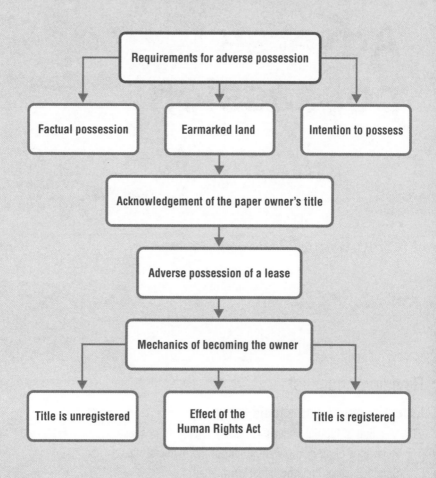

A printable version of this topic map is available from **www.pearsoned.co.uk/lawexpress**

■Introduction

The key to this topic is to go through all the stages in how title is acquired by adverse possession, logically paying particular attention to:

■ The effect of the decision in *Pye* v. *Graham* (2002) – this is a really vital case which is relevant to a number of areas: factual possession, intention to possess, possible acknowledgement of the owner's title and the effect of the Human Rights Act.

■ The mechanics of acquiring title under the LRA 2002: the stages are quite detailed, although not difficult in themselves, and can figure prominently in both essay and problem questions.

■ The position where a lease, rather than a freehold, is adversely possessed. The actual periods for which land must be adversely possessed will be explained in detail at the end of this chapter, but it will help you to understand this topic if you remember the following basic times:

■ *Registered land*: initially 10 years (it was 12 years before the LRA 2002 came into force);

■ *Unregistered land*: 12 years.

ASSESSMENT ADVICE

Essay question There are two obvious areas for an essay question:

1 A comparison between the methods of acquiring title where title to land is unregistered with where it is registered.
2 The impact of the Human Rights Act, and here a good knowledge of *Pye* v. *Graham* is essential.

Boost your marks by looking at newspaper accounts of *Pye* v. *Graham* (this case was widely reported in the national press) where the papers referred to other cases where land had been adversely possessed. This will paint a picture of the social context of the subject.

Problem question A problem question will almost certainly involve most of the areas in this chapter: the extent to which the land has been adversely possessed; the possible effect of an acknowledgement of the owner's title (marks to be gained here by appreciating that the law is not entirely clear); earmarking of the land for future use and the actual application for registration.

Do not start your answer until you have checked:

■ Dates: make a note of when possession began and the date now.

■ Is it a claim to a freehold or to a leasehold?

■ Is title to the land registered or unregistered? As always in land law, do check weather it is an alternative: on the basis that title is registered or unregistered. The rules differ considerably depending on whether title is registered or unregistered, so the first thing which you do when you see a problem question on this area is to check which category the land falls into.

■ Sample question

Could you answer this question? Below is a typical problem question that could arise on this topic. Guidelines on answering the question are included at the end of the chapter, while a sample essay question and guidance on tackling it are included on the companion website.

PROBLEM QUESTION

In 1998 Amy started to cultivate a field behind her house. She planted vegetables and later she erected a shed to store her gardening tools. Later on she also planted a hedge along the boundary to act as a windbreak. The registered owner of the field was Robert, who lived in France.

On a day visit to inspect his property Robert told Amy that he had no present use for the field but that he intended at some future time to seek planning permission to build on it. Meanwhile, he told Amy that he would be prepared to grant her a short lease. Amy told him to write to her solicitor about this but, although negotiations followed, no lease was ever granted.

Amy died in 2002, leaving all her property to her son Christopher, who had lived with her. Robert also died in 2006, leaving all his property to his daughter Sally. Sally has had poor health and lives in a nursing home.

It is now 2010 and Christopher asks your advice on whether he can be registered as owner of the field and, if so, on the procedures which will apply.

◼ Factual possession

These words of Slade J in *Powell* v. *McFarlane* (1977) were accepted by the HL in *Pye* v. *Graham* as representing the law: 'Factual possession signifies an appropriate degree of physical control ... Everything must depend on the particular circumstances but broadly, I think what must be shown ... is that the alleged possessor has been dealing with the land as an occupying owner might have been expected to deal with it and that no one else has done so.'

KEY CASE

Pye (J.A.) Oxford Ltd v. *Graham* [2002] 3 All ER 865 (HL)
Concerning: factual possession

Facts

The defendants farmed land including grazing cattle, maintained the boundary, trimmed the hedges and re-seeded the land. The paper owner had no key to the gate to the land.

Legal principle

Sufficient factual possession.

Note cases where there was no factual possession, e.g. *Tecbild* v. *Chamberlain Ltd* (1969) where playing on the land by children and tethering of ponies was not enough, and contrast with cases where there was sufficient possession, e.g. *Williams* v. *Usherwood* (1983): land was enclosed by a fence, three cars were parked on it and a driveway was paved.

EXAM TIP

Rather than learn many cases on what constitutes factual possession, it is better to be clear about what Slade J said (above) in *Powell* v. *McFarlane* and apply this to the question.

◼ Intention to possess

You need to deal with this separately from factual possession as it may be that although there is factual possession there is clearly no intention to possess.

> **Example**
>
> X is in occupation of a locked house which he has agreed to look after for a friend, while the friend is away on holiday. He may have factual possession, but he does not intend to actually possess it.

This example is from the speech of Lord Browne-Wilkinson in *Pye* v. *Graham* in which he emphasised that intention to own is not required, only intention to possess. This means that the adverse possessor (AP) does not have to prove that he believed that the land was his (he knows that it not his anyway) but that he intended to exclude the paper owner.

■ Earmarked land

This follows from the above point. Can an AP intend to possess where he is aware that the paper owner had a future intended use? It follows that he can, as it is sufficient if he intends to exclude the paper owner. The present law is now clear and easily recognised in exams. It is illustrated by the case below.

KEY CASE

Buckinghamshire County Council v. *Moran* [1989] 2 All ER 225 (CA)

Concerning: whether a claim to adverse possession can be defeated by showing that the paper owner had intended a future use for it

Facts

The defendant enclosed land belonging to the claimant and treated it as an extension of his garden. The claimant had intended to use the land to carry out a road diversion.

Legal principle

The fact that the paper owner had a future intended use for the land for a road diversion did not stop the defendant from adversely possessing it.

Make your answer stand out

You can add marks to your answer by referring to how the law reached its present position. Earlier cases had held that earmarking land for a future use could prevent adverse possession until the intended use for the land was abandoned. See *Leigh* v. *Jack* (1879) and Denning MR in *Wallis's Cayton Bay Holiday Camp Ltd* v. *Shell-Mex and BP Ltd* (1974). The latest important case in this area is *Pye* v. *Graham* (above) where the HL held that it would only be very occasionally that the fact that there is an intended future use will prevent adverse possession. Note also *Beulane Properties* v. *Palmer* (2006), where there was a (probably short-lived) attempt to reintroduce the concept of earmarking in the context of the Human Rights Act.

! **Don't be tempted to...**

Be careful that you check if land has been earmarked for future use, e.g. Jack occupied land belonging to Sarah who intended to use it at some future date as a horse-riding establishment. This earmarking of land is usually irrelevant today (see above) and so almost certainly (see *Pye* v. *Graham*) will not affect the outcome of your answer but could have prevented acquisition of title by Jack until the *Moran* case. Make this clear!

■ Acknowledgement of the paper owner's title

This point often arises in exam questions and is easily recognised.

Example

X has occupied a house belonging to Y for the past nine years and has treated it as his own. Y then says to X that he owes rent for the use of the house. An exam situation may say that either:

- X agrees to pay rent to Y; or
- X actually pays rent to Y and becomes Y's tenant.

In the second situation, X is clearly no longer an adverse possessor, as he has become Y's tenant. It is impossible to be both at the same time, otherwise all tenants would claim ownership by adverse possession.

It is the first example which has caused difficulty.

Pye v. *Graham* [2002] 3 All ER 865 (HL)

Concerning: whether willingness of the squatter to pay if asked defeats a claim to adverse possession

Facts

The defendant occupied fields owned by the claimant under a licence and when this expired the defendant asked for a further licence which the paper owners refused to grant. The defendant remained in occupation.

Legal principle

Lord Browne-Wilkinson held that 'there is no inconsistency between a squatter being willing to pay the paper owner if asked and his being in the meantime in possession'. The point is that an intention to own is not required. If it was, willingness to pay would be fatal to a claim because why should I pay someone else for what I claim to own?

Adverse possession of a lease

This presents a different problem in one way, although the basic requirements for adverse possession remain.

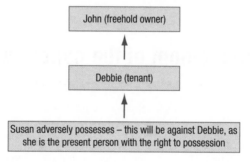

Unregistered

■ If Susan adversely possesses, she has the right to possession, but this does not end Debbie's lease, so Debbie remains liable on the lease.

■ Susan is not an assignee of the lease and so cannot be sued directly on the covenants in it.

■ If Debbie breaches the covenants in the lease, John may claim to forfeit it. This will then give John the immediate right to possession and so he can then eject Susan.

■ Time does not begin to run against John until the lease expires, but if Susan remains in possession she may, on the expiry of at least a further 12 years from the end of the lease, claim John's freehold.

■ John can also bring forward the time when he can bring possession proceedings to evict Susan by taking a surrender of the lease from Debbie (*Fairweather* v. *St Marylebone Property Co. Ltd* (1962)).

Registered

There will be a transfer of the lease as the squatter can be registered as owner of it, and so the squatter as the new tenant will be bound by the covenants in it. Meanwhile it appears that it will be possible *before* the squatter is registered as owner for the landlord to take a surrender of the lease under the principles in *Fairweather* (above). This will not be possible *after* registration as the (now) former tenant has nothing to surrender.

 Make your answer stand out

The decision in *Fairweather* v. *St Marylebone* has been controversial, although is now firmly entrenched in the law. The point is simple: how can the tenant surrender the lease when he no longer has it for practical purposes as the squatter has possession now? Look at Wade (1962).

■ Applications to be registered as proprietor: unregistered land

When the period of 12 years is completed, the AP becomes entitled to be the owner. There is no actual process as such but the AP will need to prove to whomever he sells to that he is indeed the owner. He takes the land subject to all existing rights.

■ Applications to be registered as proprietor: the scheme of the LRA 2002 (Sch. 6, LRA 2002)

By contrast with the position where title is unregistered, the new scheme has a number of safeguards for the existing proprietor. In a problem question you will first need to establish that there is a right to be registered (factual possession plus intention to possess) as this is not affected by the LRA 2002. Only after you have dealt with this should you go through the procedures under this scheme.

Note these abbreviations:

AP: adverse possessor.
RP: registered proprietor.

Summary of the above scheme

The effect is that, except in three special cases, the current RP has two years from the date on which he or she is informed of the claim of the AP to recover possession.

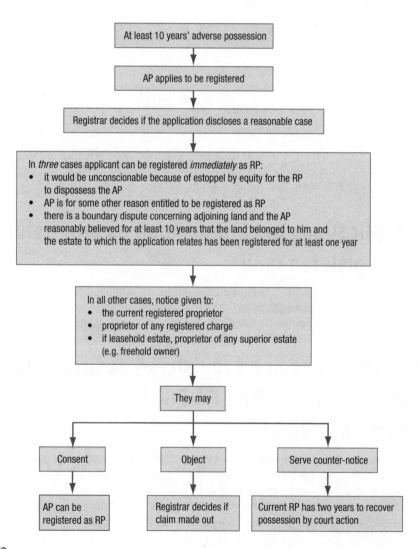

At least 10 years' adverse possession

↓

AP applies to be registered

↓

Registrar decides if the application discloses a reasonable case

↓

In *three* cases applicant can be registered *immediately* as RP:
- it would be unconscionable because of estoppel by equity for the RP to dispossess the AP
- AP is for some other reason entitled to be registered as RP
- there is a boundary dispute concerning adjoining land and the AP reasonably believed for at least 10 years that the land belonged to him and the estate to which the application relates has been registered for at least one year

↓

In all other cases, notice given to:
- the current registered proprietor
- proprietor of any registered charge
- if leasehold estate, proprietor of any superior estate (e.g. freehold owner)

↓

They may

→ Consent → AP can be registered as RP

→ Object → Registrar decides if claim made out

→ Serve counter-notice → Current RP has two years to recover possession by court action

Note the following extra points:

- No application can be made when the current RP is unable because of mental disability to either make decisions on an application or to communicate those decisions (Sch. 6, para. 8(2)). Exam questions sometimes raise this issue by telling you that the RP is ill or abroad. This does not by itself involve Sch. 6, para. 8(2).

- The AP takes subject to all existing legal and equitable rights in the land except registered charges (Sch. 6, para. 9(2) and (3)). This is why a registered chargee is entitled to be served with notice of an application so that it can object. The only exceptions are where the AP is registered as the RP in one of the three special cases above. Here he or she will take subject to the charge.

- The AP can rely on periods of possession by another AP, e.g. X adversely possesses for five years and then dies but Y, her son, who had lived with her, continues the AP (Sch. 6, para. 11, LRA 2002).

■ Adverse possession – change of squatter and paper owner

This point often appears in an exam problem question.

How to deal with this:

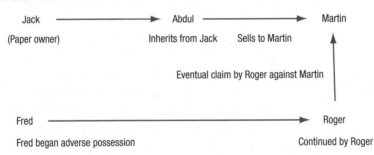

- Obviously, it is assumed that between them Fred and Roger have 10 years' adverse possession.

- This must be continuous possession.

- If so, Roger can rely on Fred's previous periods of possession (Sch. 6, para. 11, LRA 2002, and see above).

- Abdul is a donee.

- He is bound by any rights in the land and this includes rights in the course of being acquired by adverse possession – often known (although not strictly) as a mini-fee simple). As the disposition to him was not for valuable consideration, it is governed by s. 28 of the LRA 2002.

REVISION NOTE

Go to Chapter 2 and check that you know exactly why Abdul's rights are governed by s. 28, LRA 2002.

■ Roger is a purchaser. His rights are governed by s. 29 of the LRA 2002.

REVISION NOTE

Go to Chapter 2 and check that you know exactly why Roger's rights are governed by s. 29.

■ Any rights in the course of being acquired by adverse possession count as overriding interests under Sch. 3, para. 2, LRA 2002, so the question is whether Roger is actually bound – would his occupation have been obvious on a reasonably careful inspection? Did Roger fail to disclose it when he could have been reasonably been expected to?

REVISION NOTE

Check overriding interests under Sch. 3, para. 2, LRA 2002: it is absolutely vital that you apply this point! See Chapter 2.

Watch for where the AP has completed the requisite period of possession before the commencement of the LRA 2002 on 13 October 2003.

Example

John began to adversely possess land belonging to Michael in 1990. By 13 October 2003, John will have completed the required period of adverse possession whether the title is registered (basic period of 12 years) or unregistered (12 years).

This point may still occur in exam questions, as a claim based on adverse possession may be made some years after the basic period for possession has been completed.

Therefore:

■ **Registered land**. John (the AP) is entitled to be registered as the proprietor of the registered estate (Sch. 12, para. 18(1), LRA 2002). Pending registration, his rights override any subsequent disposition of the registered estate, provided that he is in actual occupation (s. 29(1) and Sch. 3, para. 2, LRA 2002).

■ **Unregistered land**. John's rights override any first registration of the land provided that, again, John is in actual occupation. If he is no longer in occupation, John's rights bind a first registered proprietor with notice of them (s. 11(4)(c), LRA 2002).

Make your answer stand out

Prepare for an essay question on the justification for the law on adverse possession. Read Dockray (1985) who looks at the justifications for allowing acquisition by adverse possession and then at the Law Commission Paper 254, 'Land Registration for the 21st century'. You should then link this with the discussion on the effect of the Human Rights Act on this area of the law (see below).

■ Effect of the Human Rights Act (HRA)

The relevant part of the ECHR (enshrined in the HRA) is Article 1 of the First Protocol: you should know all of it but the vital part here is: 'No one shall be deprived of the peaceful enjoyment of his possessions except in the public interest and subject to the conditions provided for by law and the general principles of international law.'

In *J.A. Pye* (*Oxford*) *Ltd* v. *UK* (2007) (see above for facts) the Grand Chamber of the ECtHR held that UK law does not infringe the ECHR and found that adverse possession was a justified control of use of land rather than a deprivation of possession and this was within the margin of appreciation. In *Ofulue* v. *Bossert* (2008) the CA followed this reasoning and held that the principles of adverse possession law were compliant with human rights law.

 Make your answer stand out

An essay question may ask you to consider the law of adverse possession in its wider social context. Read Cobb and Fox (2007) 'Living outside the system? The (im)morality of urban squatting after the Land Registration Act 2002'. The actual decision of the ECtHR in *Pye* is considered by Kerridge and Brierley (2007) in 'Adverse possession, human rights and land registration: and they all lived happily ever after?'

■Chapter summary: putting it all together

Test yourself

- ☐ Can you tick all the points from the **revision checklist** at the beginning of this chapter?
- ☐ Attempt the **sample question** from the beginning of this chapter using the answer guidelines below.
- ☐ Go to the **companion website** to access more revision support online, including interactive quizzes, sample questions with answer guidelines, 'you be the marker' exercises, flashcards and podcasts you can download.

Answer guidelines

See problem question at the start of the chapter. A diagram illustrating how to structure your answer is available on the companion website.

Approaching the question

This question involves a number of issues all revolving around adverse possession. Make sure that you deal with all in full as none of them are particularly difficult in themselves and so you could pick up a really good mark.

Important points to include

- Begin by checking dates and whether title is registered: it is, so initial period of 10 years and here it is now 2010 and Amy's possession began in 1998.
- Now check if Amy had factual possession and intention to possess for this time: look carefully at facts and compare with cases. May be doubtful whether she has, but note that it is now 13 years since Amy began the acts, which together may amount to possession. The planting of the hedge was later.
- Significance of negotiations for lease: note *Pye* v. *Graham*.
- Deal with relevance of earmarking.
- Christopher takes over Amy's claim: Sch. 6, para. 11, LRA 2002.
- Sally inherits the land: s. 28, LRA 2002.

- Sally's health: Sch. 6, para. 8(2), LRA 2002.
- Application for registration: procedures in Sch. 6, LRA 2002.

 Make your answer stand out

Discuss the possible impact of the Human Rights Act (HRA) – see *Pye* v. *Graham* and the discussion above and make sure that you actually relate the question to the HRA and do not just mention it!

READ TO IMPRESS

Cobb and Fox, 'Living outside the system? The (im)morality of urban squatting after the Land Registration Act 2002' (2007) 27 LS 236.

Dockray, 'Why do we need adverse possession?' [1985] Conv 272.

Kerridge and Brierley, 'Adverse possession, human rights and land registration: and they all lived happily ever after?' [2007] Conv 552.

Law Commission Paper 254, 'Land registration for the 21st century' paras 10.5–10.9.

Wade, 'Landlords, tenants and squatters' (1962) 78 LQR 541.

NOTES

NOTES

And finally, before the exam ...

As you come to the end of your revision, remember:

- Land law exams *do not* require you to recall vast numbers of cases.
- Land law exams *do* require you to be accurate and precise. This means that you must be absolutely clear about the point of a case.

Test yourself

☐ Look at the **revision checklists** at the start of each chapter. Are you happy that you can now tick them all? If not, go back to the particular chapter and work through the material again. If you are still struggling, seek help from your tutor.

☐ Go to the **companion website** and revisit the online resources.

    ☐ Take the full **study plan** test to assess your knowledge in all areas.

    ☐ Try the **practice quizzes** and see if you can score full marks for each chapter.

    ☐ Attempt to answer the **sample questions** for each chapter within the time limit.

    ☐ Use the **flashcards** to test your recall of the legal principles of the cases and statutes you've revised and the definitions of important terms.

    ☐ See if you can spot the strengths and weaknesses of the samples answers in '**you be the marker**'.

    ☐ Listen to the podcast and then attempt the question it discusses.

☐ Make sure that you take into account the different levels of knowledge required for essays and problem questions in tort. Problem questions require that you state and apply the current law whilst essays require far greater depth of knowledge.

☐ Follow up some of the suggested reading to ensure that you have the necessary level of understanding to tackle an essay question and impress your examiner.

■ Linking it all up

Remember the 'Land law box' in the Introduction? You may wish to revisit this and make sure that you understand how each part fits together. When revising, it is important not to leave out the fundamentals of the subject.

For instance, if you leave out registered land when revising and you decide to concentrate only on easements, adverse possession, and leases, you will find that when you come to these topics you immediately run up against land registration principles, e.g. is the lease an overriding interest? Does an equitable easement have to be registered? How does an adverse possessor become registered? You cannot answer these questions without knowledge of the principles of registered land. Remember, too, that questions have a nasty habit of asking you if it would make any difference to your answer if the title was unregistered, so you also need to know this. And of course, you cannot escape knowing the difference between the legal and equitable interests in Chapter 1.

Check where there are overlaps between subject areas (you may want to review the 'Revision note' boxes throughout this book). Make a careful note of these, as knowing how one topic may lead into another can increase your marks significantly. Here are some examples:

✓ Creation of rights over land

✓ Leases and licences

✓ Easements and profits

You might want to go back over each chapter and review these areas, and also look for other possible overlapping rights.

■ Sample question

Below is a problem question that incorporates overlapping areas of the law. See if you can answer this question, drawing upon your knowledge of the whole subject area. Guidelines on answering this question are included at the end of this section.

PROBLEM QUESTION

Last month Susan bought an office block with two acres of ground from Aidan. It is freehold with registered title. Since her purchase, the following matters have come to light:

- Egbert tells Susan that Aidan allowed him to park his caravan on the land and he intends to continue doing this.

- Sally has come round and produced a letter from Aidan telling her that she could store materials in a shed which is also used as a store by Aidan.

- Louise has produced an agreement signed by Aidan giving a lease of two rooms in the block. The lease is to last for two years and is to commence next month.

- Arthur tells Susan that he has taken over a corner of the field to use for car repairs. He says that he started doing this 10 years ago and that Aidan never took any notice.

Advise Sally on whether she is bound by any of these claims and what other action, if any, she should take.

Would your answer differ if title was unregistered?

Answer guidelines

Approaching the question

- Note that title is registered. Check Chapter 2 for both registered land and unregistered land.

- Remember the drill: check what right it is and then decide if it has been validly created.

- Remember that land law is a jigsaw. Make sure that the pieces do fit!

- See if a situation might involve a possible overlap between different possible estates and interests in land.

Important points to include

Egbert: Easement of parking? (See Chapter 8.) If so, then no evidence of a deed or written agreement so cannot be an express easement, but has it been acquired by prescription? Apply different rules for registered and unregistered land.

Sally: Is this a lease or a licence? If a licence, will not bind Sally – see Chapters 5 and 6. If unregistered, same answer as a licence does not create a proprietary interest. If a lease, then ask whether it is legal or equitable and, having decided this, ask whether in either case it could bind Susan. Consider whether it could be an easement and if not, why not.

Louise: This is a lease, but is it validly granted? Will s. 54(1), LPA apply? May be equitable. Again, apply different rules for registered and unregistered land and check Chapter 1 for creation of equitable interests.

Arthur: Possible claim to title by adverse possession – see Chapter 10 – has there been both factual possession and intention to possess? Distinguish between periods where title registered and unregistered.

 Make your answer stand out

- Refer in the Egbert and Sally situations to the Law Commission's proposals on easements, and estimate how they might affect this answer if they were implemented.
- Detailed discussion of whether an equitable lease in the Sally situation can bind a purchaser. This point is often badly dealt with.
- Mention the Human Rights Act in the Arthur situation.

NOTES

Glossary of terms

The glossary is divided into two parts: key definitions and other useful terms. The key definitions can be found within the chapter in which they occur as well as here, below. These definitions are the essential terms that you must know and understand in order to prepare for an exam. The additional list of terms provides further definitions of useful terms and phrases which will also help you answer examination and coursework questions effectively. These terms are highlighted in the text as they occur but the definition can only be found here.

■ Key definitions

Bare licences	Licences given without any consideration from the licensee, i.e. when you are invited to someone's house for a party.
Borrower and lender in a mortgage	Borrower is the mortgagor and the lender in a mortgage is the mortgagee.
Contractual licence	Where a licence is given for valuable consideration.
Corporeal hereditaments	The land and what is attached to the land.
Easement	Confers the right to use the land of another in some way or to prevent it from being used for certain purposes, e.g. rights of way and rights of water and light.
Equitable interests	Are not binding on a bona fide purchaser for value without notice.
Equitable	Means that the right was originally only recognised by the Court of Chancery, which dealt with equitable rights, and not by the Courts of Common Law.
Estate in land	Refers to the rights which a person has to control and use the land. An estate owner is often called the owner of the land.
Estoppel	Arises where one person (the representee) has been led to act on the representation of another (the representor).

If so, and if the representee then acts to his/her detriment on the basis of this promise, then in equity the court may grant the representative a remedy.

Fee simple absolute in possession
Fee – can be inherited.

Simple – by anyone.

Absolute – will not end on a certain event, i.e. to X until he marries.

In possession – not e.g. to X at 21.

Fixtures and fittings
Fixtures are objects which are fixed to the land in such a way as to be part of it. Fittings are not.

Incorporeal hereditaments
Rights over land. Section 205(1)(ix) of the LPA 1925 provides that it means 'an easement, right, privilege, or benefit in, over, or derived from land'.

Injunction
A court order which either orders a lawful act to be done or restrains an unlawful act.

Interest in land
A right which a person has over another's land.

Joint tenancy
Where there are no shares, i.e. all the joint tenants own all the land jointly.

Land
'Land ... and mines and minerals, whether or not held apart from the surface' – land is not just the actual surface but also land below and air space above. What is unsettled is how far it extends: the old phrase '*usque ad coelum et ad inferos*' (up to heaven and down to hell) is legally incorrect but the landowner does own at least some portion, otherwise it would be impossible to dig the ground and to erect a block of flats. Note *Bernstein* v. *Skyviews and General Ltd* (1978): claim by a landowner for trespass in respect of flights over his house for aerial photography rejected: the court held that a landowner only owns such airspace necessary for the reasonable enjoyment of the land.

Legal interests
Are binding on all the world, i.e. everyone who buys the land.

Licence
Permission from an owner of land (licensor) to the licensee to use the land for a specific purpose.

Licence coupled with a grant
Where the licence is linked to an interest in the land, e.g. a licence to go on to land to collect wood. The right to collect wood is a profit.

Misrepresentation
An untrue statement of fact which induces a person to enter into a transaction.

Mortgage	A charge on land to secure a debt.
Negative covenant	One which restricts the use to which land can be put.
Overreaching	The process by which equitable rights which exist under a trust of land are removed from the land and transferred to the money (called capital money) which has just been paid to purchase the land. The effect is to give the purchaser automatic priority over equitable interests under a trust.
Overriding interest	An unregistered disposition which overrides registered dispositions.
Personal rights	Those which are not capable of binding third parties, i.e. licences.
Prescription	Acquisition of easements and profits by long use.
Profit	Gives the right to take something from the land of another, e.g. peat, fish, wood or grazing rights.
Proprietary rights	Those which are capable of binding third parties, i.e. legal estates and legal and equitable interests in land.
Protected registered interests	Any interests which are not overriding and include: restrictive covenants; legal and equitable easements and profits; estate contracts; and rights of beneficiaries under a trust.
Registrable disposition	One that must be completed by registration.
Rentcharge	Gives the owner the right to a periodical sum of money secured on land independently of any lease or mortgage.
Restrictive covenant	Where a person covenants in a deed not to use his land in a certain way or to do something on his land, e.g. to keep fences in repair or not to build on the land.
Specific performance	A court order which commands the performance of a contract.
Tenancy at will	Where the tenant, with the owner's consent, occupies land at the will of the owner who, therefore, may terminate it at any time. The tenant has no security of tenure and is really in no better position than a licensee.
Tenancy in common	Where the beneficial owners have shares in the land.
Tenant at sufferance	Where the tenant, after the expiry of the lease, continues in possession without the consent of the landlord (remember that a tenant at will does have consent). A tenant at sufferance has no real tenancy and cannot even a sue another for trespass.

Term of years absolute   (In relation to a lease) any period having a fixed and certain duration. 'Absolute' appears to have no meaning beyond the fact that a term of years may be absolute even if it contains a clause enabling either party to determine it by notice.

Trust   Arises when property is held by one person (the trustee) on trust for another (the beneficiary).

■ Other useful terms

Assignment   Transfer of property such as, in land law, a lease.

Beneficiaries   Those who are entitled in equity to property which is held on trust and who therefore have the equitable (beneficial) interest in that property.

Commonhold   A method of holding freehold land used to enable the owners of flats to form a company which will hold the common parts (e.g. the stairs) as commonhold.

Covenant   An obligation contained in a deed.

Deed   An instrument which makes it clear on its face that it is intended to be a deed and which satisfies the requirements for execution as a deed.

Equity   The body of rules developed and administered by the Court of Chancery.

Freehold   A legal estate in land which lasts for an unlimited time and in practice is perpetual and which today is held in fee simple absolute in possession.

Leasehold   A legal estate which lasts for a definite time and is today held as a term of years absolute.

Obiter   An observation made in a judgment which is not part of the actual decision in the case and so is not a precedent (in full, obiter dicta) but is often used a guide to what the law might be.

Paper owner   The holder of the legal title to land which is being adversely possessed.

Periodic tenancy   A tenancy for a certain period (weekly, monthly quarterly, etc.) which is automatically renewed at the end of each period unless either party gives notice.

Power of attorney   A person (attorney) is appointed to make decisions on behalf of another (donor) or to act on behalf of another.

GLOSSARY OF TERMS

Registered proprietor The person who is registered as the proprietor of land to which the title has been registered.

Rentcharge A sum, payable at periodic intervals, which is charged on freehold land.

Severance Where something is divided up, e.g. where a joint tenancy is divided into separate shares so that it becomes a tenancy in common.

Trustees Those who hold property on trust for others who are the beneficiaries.

Index